1 MONTH OF
FREE
READING

at
www.ForgottenBooks.com

By purchasing this book you are
eligible for one month membership to
ForgottenBooks.com, giving you
unlimited access to our entire
collection of over 1,000,000 titles via
our web site and mobile apps.

To claim your free month visit:
www.forgottenbooks.com/free34912

ISBN 978-0-483-79671-3
PIBN 10034912

o

THE DESERTED CITY;

EVA,

A Tale in Two Cantos;

AND OTHER POEMS.

BY

JOSEPH BOUNDEN.

LONDON :

PRINTED FOR LONGMAN, HURST, REES, ORME,
BROWN, AND GREEN.

1824.

LONDON:

Printed by D. S. Maurice, Fenchurch Street.

TO

THOMAS MOORE, ESQ.

AUTHOR OF LALLA ROOKH,
IRISH MELODIES,
&c. &c.

SIR,

You have kindly permitted me to present this volume to the public, under the protection of your name—a name among the highest on the roll of living Poets. I hope the malice of criticism will not subject my work to any comparison whatever with any of his, who has condescended thus to adorn it. If the public should pronounce it in the least degree worthy of a sanction so illustrious, it will surpass the highest ambition of,

SIR,

Your sincere Admirer,

and

Very humble servant,

THE AUTHOR.

PREFACE.

THE Publication of a volume of Poems has been deemed one of the most venturous of literary attempts.—If it were so formerly, the hazard is now fearfully increased, by the list of bright names to be encountered in this department of genius : and a new claimant is fortunate indeed if he succeed in obtaining notice, when the productions of Moore, and Byron, and Campbell, and Rogers, and Scott, and Southey, and other great minds, are lying on the table of every library. But soldiers will go upon the forlorn hope—even so will poets write! I might plead the solicitations of friends—repeated promises of compliance—and what is more, if it constitute a plea, my own inclination—but with these things the public have nothing to do : their right is to judge of works by their own merit, and this, sooner or later, they seldom fail to perform. I ask for no favour beyond what the production may be fairly entitled to; and therefore, to the decisions of fair and impartial criticism, I shall bow with the deference due to its authority; but any censure arising from motives other than those which ought to operate in pronouncing sentence upon a production of the mind, I shall treat with the contempt such motives deserve. Should I be asked where I lay the supposed scene of the Deserted City?—I answer, the reader may place it where he pleases; I may have described, perhaps, the scenes most familiar to myself; but it does not therefore follow that the sentiment is applicable to that spot only. As long as there are Cities to be destroyed by war and tyranny, it will have but too many "a local habitation and a name." In this Poem, I own I have not aimed at flights of imagination; I was more anxious to paint realities, and to describe the evil, and its causes. Whether in so doing I have done well or ill, is for the public to judge. In Eva I have allowed a greater latitude to imagination, and it is perhaps necessarily the more poetical. The lines on Electricity were written for an anniversary of a literary institution;* for which occasion, such a subject

* The Philomathic Institution, Burton Street, Burton Crescent. The Author embraces this opportunity of testifying his gratitude to his fellow members, for much personal kindness and friendship.

was deemed at least appropriate, however unpoetical the theme might sound; though I believe there is more poetry in science than most people are aware of. It is one of a series of poems on scientific subjects, which, if the writer find time and ability, may, at a future time, be completed. To my distinguished Dedicatee and my friends, I owe an apology that the Poems are not better— to the public any such apology would be impertinent.

J. B.

London, Feb. 1824.

CONTENTS.

THE

DESERTED CITY.

PART I.

DESERTED CITY.

PART I.

PROUD Urburgh! once fam'd city of this land,
Where golden ease repaid th' industrious hand;
Where commerce flourish'd, and where learning grew;
And wealth, and taste, and grandeur, charm'd the view;
Where life in all its joys and sorrows past,
Guarded by power that promised long to last;
Where fickle fashions daily lur'd the sight,
And noisy mirth disturb'd the sleep of night;
Where scenes of splendour fir'd the blazing square,
Sought by the great, and crowded by the fair:
Thou seat of elegance, and every art
That could delight, seduce, or mend the heart:
So late in glory tow'ring to the skies,
How art thou fallen now, no more to rise!

B

In splendid ruin still alive to fame,
Thy giant wreck shall long preserve thy name!

Memory, awake! amidst thy stores retrace
The former bustle of this lonely place;
There, as in life, I view the motley crowd,
In hurry and confusion swift and loud :—
The fools of fashion, idolizing dress—
The tatter'd form that wither'd in distress—
The idle loiterers that loung'd along—
The group that listen'd to the minstrel's song—
The Postman hast'ning with his letter'd store,
Oft watch'd by anxious eyes from door to door,
Whose sacred charge of business—friendship—love—
A source of sorrow or delight would prove—
To wake distress—despair—or bid them cease;
Herald of ill—or messenger of peace:
Or warm with all th' affection of the heart,
That fate had doom'd from all it lov'd to part.
The active Tradesman, jostling through the street,
Who scarce could stop a passing friend to greet—
Boys, seeking play in ev'ry roomy spot,
The stern command to hasten, heeded not—
The prancing steed, whose eye shot fire around,

Whose iron tread flash'd o'er the flinty ground—
The crowd around some casual scene of woe,
Where few reliev'd what many sought to know—
And children following each unusual sight,
Gazing with vacant wonder and delight!
How often have I seen the hurrying throng,
In ceaseless line, these pavements pass along;
As if the world had urg'd her myriads here,
As to a spot unknown to pain and fear.
How often have I heard, with echoing feet
The sons of labour tread the twilight street;
Or caught the sigh of friendless, houseless woe,
Crouch'd at a door, or wand'ring faint and slow.
Oft, at that early hour, each fabric round
Shook with the waggons grating on the ground,
That slowly brought the gifts of Ceres' hand
To feed th' insatiate mistress of the land;
While chariots rattling as they roll'd along,
Bore the last lingerers from the festive throng.

Here oft returning from the social board,
Where friendship all its inspiration pour'd,
With mind at once enliven'd and reliev'd,
And by the rapid flight of time deceiv'd,—

Homeward I trod each solitary street,
Whose silence echo'd to my hast'ning feet.
Perchance around the full orb'd, welcome Moon,
Pour'd from the arch of heaven night's silver noon;
Then, as I past, the shadow'd domes I trac'd,
And o'er reflected roofs and turrets pac'd;
And walls and spires, that seem'd my path to pave,
Like sails and masts upon the moonlight wave!

Here oft, with feelings that can ne'er return,
I view'd the hero's tomb—the patriot's urn—
The vast Cathedral, solemn to the eye—
The trophied column tow'ring to the sky—
The House rever'd where senates held debate,
On whose decisions hung the nation's fate;
For whom, alas! that rev'rence lives no more;
'Tis now but to remember—and deplore!
There love of power and lust of gold inspir'd,
And left but few with patriot virtue fir'd:
And thence the nation first receiv'd the blow
That laid her hopes, and strength, and glories low.
Its less'ning line of arch the bridge still shows,
And o'er the wave it's giant shadow throws,
Though scarce a lonely wand'rer hails its view,

Nor vessel stoops her sail while gliding through.

Here stood a home to shield the poor and old,
Where childhood play'd, and age long stories told—
Where some who trod the busy paths of life,
In sorrow clos'd it's round of care and strife;
Whose past bright days, in bitter contrast brought,
Form'd the last efforts of expiring thought!
Collected here the wreck of human kind—
The shatter'd frame, and the exhausted mind;
The hopeless spirit, and the sunder'd heart,
By anguish and misfortune wrench'd apart—
In ev'ry stage of slow or swift decay,
Past the dim hours of life's autumnal day;
Falling like dry and yellow leaves around,
And soon, like them, to mingle with the ground!
There musing melancholy silent sate,
Pond'ring the dark vicissitudes of fate;
And brooding on the past in madd'ning thought,
When life with hope and energy was fraught.
There nerveless palsy shook her trembling head,
And hoary childhood prest his constant bed—
There the half maniac mus'd his dreaming day,
And idiotism laugh'd its life away!

And thence the young, of parentage unknown,
With hopes, and fears, and feelings all their own,
Launch'd out on life's rough sea, unaided and alone!

The scenes where pleasure held her fairy reign,
And bound the laughing groups in flow'ry chain;
From whom th' unnumber'd hours too swiftly fled—
For whom too soon the morn its twilight shed—
The floor which beauty press'd in mazy dance,
And blest her followers with a casual glance—
The lounge where idlers stroll'd away a noon,
And walks where lovers whisper'd to the Moon—
The tasteful shops that lin'd the crowded street,
And busy docks that hail'd th' approaching fleet—
The public gallery of cherish'd art,
Whose beauties soften'd and sublim'd the heart—
The palace where the monarch sat enthron'd,
And the barr'd prison where the felon groan'd—
All—all are fall'n! and desolation reigns,
Where flourish'd once the mistress of the plains!

Urburgh! thy suburbs were a scene of joy
The morrow's doubtful ills could not destroy!
When summer evening rob'd the gorgeous sky,

And day was loveliest as it fled the eye,
Passing away in many a crimson streak,
Like the last flush on dying beauty's cheek,—
The fields were crowded by a mingled throng,
The young, the gay, the active, and the strong.
There careless boys, and men releas'd from care,
In varied pastime, woo'd the evening air—
There life exhibited her brightest face,
And thoughtless pleasure laugh'd in ev'ry place—
There, ere the Moon her snowy radiance shed,
Linger'd the student ere he sought his bed—
And there the servant, loos'd from masters' chain,
Awhile forgot that servitude was pain.
While merchants urg'd their dusty wheels from town,
To breathe the country air on beds of down,
Children in groups were homeward seen to creep,
With lagging steps and eyes half clos'd in sleep;
Or mark'd with sorrow that th' approach of night
Had shut the sport so early from their sight.

Then, Urburgh! glorious was thy perfect day;
Along thy river's banks what navies lay,
To waft the produce of thy land away;
Or laden with the fruits of other shores,

To feed thy luxuries and swell thy stores.
Thy roads, like rays that from a centre fly,
To ev'ry point diverging, met the eye:
Whence all the country pour'd its wealth to town,
And constant traffic rattled up and down.
From thence th' approaching rustics with amaze
Turn'd on thy numerous spires their eager gaze;
And urg'd with anxious haste their steps along,
To view thy wonders, and to join thy throng.
What bustle did thy crowded inns display,
Where ceaseless business claim'd the restless day.
How rich thy streets! where trade, to lure the eye,
And tempt the wealthy as they loiter'd by,
Brought from all climes, to one capacious mart,
The gifts of nature, and the works of art—
The glitt'ring metals, shap'd unnumber'd ways,
And jewels darting all their varied rays;
And robes, the rich and lovely to adorn,
Whose fashions liv'd a night, and died at morn—
All pride, caprice, or fancy could require;
And all that pamper'd sense could e'en desire;
The sails of commerce wafted o'er the main,
From Arctic seas, and India's sultry plain;
Earth's farthest realms, at thy supreme command,

Yielded their stores to deck thy golden land.
When day-light sunk behind the western shore,
Thy lights appear'd a second day to pour;
Whose countless rays, reflected on the eye,
Seem'd like a distant fire that blush'd on high,
And almost chas'd the darkness from the sky.

Here all was intellectual—glowing—bright!
No winter of the soul—no dearth—no night!
Earth had no wisdom that was stranger here—
In art no rival—and in joy no peer.
The land's etherial part; in sanguine hour,
Here came each fiery soul, and rose to power;
Till science soaring reach'd her highest aim,
And pour'd o'er all the world a mental flame.
The country seem'd but made to yield the best
Of art and nature to adorn her crest;
The willing slave to spread her ample board,
With all the field, the garden, could afford.
Howe'er the peasant lov'd his sunny scene,
Boasted his cloudless skies, and verdant green,
Once cherish'd here, he slighted, or forgot,
The listless quiet of the lowly cot;
And found his soul in spell of magic bound,

By more intense delights that spread around.
For him the silent glen had charms no more,
He came to wonder—tarried to adore!
There life was sameness—here 'twas ever new,
With fresh excitement op'ning on his view—
There lack of thought had dimm'd his vacant hours,
While here his soul had scope for all her powers.

Yes, beauty o'er the rural prospect reigns,
Clothes the fair fields, and brightens all the plains.
'Tis joy to breathe the pure and fragrant air,
And see the sun revel in glory there;
To view the clouds in fairy form and hue,
And the fields glitt'ring in a sea of dew;
To see the yellow morn its wings unfold,
And ev'ning set in crimson and in gold;
To tread the silent dell in pensive mood,
And stray by moonlight through the thoughtful wood;
To be in solitude, but scarce alone,
Circled by forms that still are fancy's own;
To climb the mountain wild, and see below
The landscape stretching in the sunny glow,
Till, fading in the horizon's misty blue,
It seems to melt in clouds, and dies from view;

To hear the distant hum—the murm'ring stream,
And wander lost in many a joyous dream :
These are high pleasures, and who feels them not,
Who views creation as a blank, or blot,
Must own a soul of cold and midnight form,
That thought can never thrill, nor feeling warm.
But still these beauties pall upon the sense;
The sated mind asks something more intense;
Some more etherial, intellectual scope,
To rouse the fancy, and inspire with hope;
To wake—to fire—to agitate the soul,
Until she burn and revel past controul;
Sweeping her own-created empire round,
That owns no law, acknowledges no bound—
But, unsubstantial as herself, displays
Unearthly scenes in fancy's brightest blaze!
And hence she flies, where kindred minds inspire,
And still in cities lights up all her fire.

Here, while the spendthrift met a summer friend,
And many a syren lur'd him to his end;
The sons of art inspiring favor found,
And saw their toils with wealth and honor crown'd :
And here, rewarded by the public hand,

The man of genius felt his powers expand ;
Heard his proud country echo with his name,
And left life's last—best gift—a deathless fame !
And here his eloquence the speaker pour'd
To breathless crowds, who listen'd and ador'd:
Now softly flowing like the glassy stream—
Now loud as angry seas th' impetuous theme !
With stormy passions then the breast he fir'd,
Or souls with love of liberty inspir'd ;
Then with deep pathos forc'd the melting sigh,
And drew the tear in many an answering eye.

Here, when the day approach'd its welcome close,
And wearied tradesmen gave their minds repose ;
Where the snug Tavern spread its seats around,
And cheerful fire, and lively groups were found
Each smiling met his neighbour and his friend,
A social hour, releas'd from care, to spend :
Where evening stole in varied talk away,
And mirth and friendship sped the parting day.
The fancied soldier plann'd lost fields to win,
Though he ne'er heard the battle's distant din :
While politicians held prolong'd debates,
And managed in idea mighty states ;

Glad, as the horn proclaim'd the newsman near,
Some fresh accounts from foreign climes to hear;
To judge who next might break a despot's yoke;
What army strike some scarce expected stroke;
Turning their arms that liberty to aid,
That tyrants hoped was vanquish'd or betray'd.
Some conn'd what taxes next would press the land,
And wrest the fruits of labor from the hand :
Whether the peace they pray'd would e'er return ;
Man cease to slaughter man, or cities burn.
There the pretended patriot found his due;
And public measures met severe review :
The Prince himself, in censure nothing spar'd,
Had there his follies or his crimes declar'd.
The wiser few discours'd of nature's laws,
Of operations, and effect, and cause ;
While shafts of wit, in harmless strife assail'd,
And manly sense, and tow'ring thought prevail'd.
Then, too, (when day went down in gold and pink,)
When some were met to talk, and some to drink;
Dress'd for the night, the noble and the fair
Sought the gay scene in chariot and in chair ;
Where taste and wealth conspir'd to yield delight,
And cards and concerts wing'd away the night;

Where life's refinement strove its best to shew,
And man the brightest polish man can know.

When welcome Sunday brought the lab'rer rest,
And shed its peace in many a weary breast—
(Sole morn that does not break on care and strife—
Toil's halcyon dawn—the holiday of life !)
On that blest day, in all their best array'd,
Th' industrious poor their virtuous pride display'd.
For six long, joyless suns in gloom immers'd,
The rescued race in field and street dispers'd ;
Leaving their humble homes, with laughing eye,
To breathe pure air, and see a brighter sky.
The modest wife hung on her husband's arm,
With every virtue grac'd, and every charm ;
Glad to embrace a summer hour to roam,
And leave her sorrows and her cares at home :
While sporting round their path their children trod,
Freed from the terrors of the tyrant rod !
That day were seen the humble and the high,
Alike ambitious of the public eye ;
In whose gay promenade 'twere hard to tell
Which in the mansion or the cot might dwell.
Propitious day ! a holiday to all !

A heaven to those who own'd religion's call!
Had no divine command that day design'd
To rest the limb, and sooth by pray'r the mind;
Still would I honor with the meed of praise
The man, who rescued from life's stormy days
Those welcome intervals of rest and peace,
When labor sleeps, and care and bustle cease;
That, like the springs amidst a desert plain,
Refresh the traveller for his toil again;
That break life's long, dull uniformity,
And set awhile the prison'd spirit free!
Like verdant isles along the ocean spread,
Or streams of light o'er clouds of darkness shed;
It dawns upon the lab'ring multitude,
An ever-look'd for, never-failing good!
Each day, whose darkness makes it doubly dear,
Seems but to struggle on to bring it near;
It comes like friendship to the captive's cell—
And for its little season—all is well!
And though like joy it swiftly glide away—
The next can scarce be thought a distant day.
Beneath each dome, where men their God ador'd,
What melting eloquence the preacher pour'd!
The guilty heart was shaken in its seat;

And seem'd to rend the breast in which it beat;

And tears—unbidden tears—suffus'd the eyes

That lately flash'd defiance at the skies.

While some implor'd the wicked to repent—

Others, on doubtful points of doctrine bent,

In mystery's mazes led and lost the mind,

That in the labyrinth no path could find.

The wiser part would man's clear duties teach,

And heaven's sublime and plain commandments preach:

Declare its doom when harden'd sinners die—

And lead the penitent to bliss on high:

Chusing the solemn and appropriate hour,

To blend instruction with religion's power;

While mute attention list'ning crowds bestow'd,

Whose hearts were melted and whose bosoms glow'd!

When o'er the sense the spell of music stole,

Seraphic rapture fir'd the rising soul!

A sacred flame through mortal fibres ran;

And heavenly feelings thrill'd the breast of man!

But now the prayer is hush'd! the hearers fled—

The worship ended, and devotion dead:

Such is the boon that discord leaves below;

Her tread an earthquake and her visit woe.

Mistaken statesmen! who on wars rely,
And to ambition all your powers apply,
In vain you boast your king's—your country's good,
While wasteful of her treasure and her blood:
In vain your armies vanquish distant coasts,
Your country's vigour dies 'midst all her boasts:
How vain—while healthful labor quits her fields—
How vain the trophies ev'ry conquest yields;
How worse than vain th' unprofitable show,
That paves the way for want, and chains, and woe!
The source of strength declines unseen away;
E'en the throne sinks in slow but sure decay:
The nation's wealth feeds many a distant shore;
Her men return to till her fields no more:
Accumulated debt o'erwhelms the state;
And dark corruption hastens on her fate.
Coercion then but fans the people's ire;
That, smother'd, kindles for a fiercer fire!
And taxes, wrung from toil's unwilling hand,
Drain the last blood-drop from a wither'd land!
Then—whether myriads, toil for bread in vain,
Till madden'd by despair, and want, and pain;
Or lifeless grandeur deck th' unpeopled ground,
Whelm'd in vast ruin falls the nation round,

And hostile bands devouring sweep along,
Fir'd with the thoughts of many a former wrong !
Or slav'ry binds the realm in hopeless chains ;
Or lawless anarchy in riot reigns.
Whate'er the means—destruction waits the land—
And thousands perish by the vengeful hand !
Thus when besieging armies circle round,
And doom some towering fortress to the ground—
The miner saps the seat of strength below,
And tottering leaves the unsubstantial show—
Still proudly frown the towers and massive walls—
Till burst in wreck the baseless fabric falls !
Whose heaps of ruins, in their giant length
Speak its past glory and its former strength !

Ah ! ye, who rashly hurl the brands of war !
And toil to feed its flames in realms afar !
Who doom mankind to death and anguish there ;
And destine realms to famine and despair !
Do ye not shudder at the tales of woe ?
Does there no tear, when cities perish, flow ?
Ye who at home in lux'ry sit, and plan
The fall of states, the agony of man—
Does fancy never picture to your souls

Corses that blacken in the flame that rolls?
Do ye ne'er dream you hear your victim's cries—
Nor see their restless shades in terror rise?
Does placid pleasure smile around your heads?
Is peace the guardian angel of your beds?
How long to you shall men their reason yield?
For your base passions seek the murd'rous field?
Devote their kind to all the woes of strife;
And dash away the little term of life?

Now let me turn my lonely wand'ring feet
Amidst yon ruins of a noble street!
What melancholy silence slumbers here,
Where busy tumult lately fill'd the ear.
Day-dreaming owls in desert chambers sleep;
And birds obscene thro' useless temples sweep—
Halls that resounded to the voice of bliss,
Now but reverberate the serpent's hiss!
Th' untrodden pavement, all with grass o'ergrown,
Shrouds reptile myriads curl'd beneath each stone.
No feet, save mine, remain to tread the ground;
No other voice invades the still profound;
Nor neighing steed, nor rattling wheel is heard;
Nor midnight sound, except the shrieking bird:

No more the proud Cathedral's deep-ton'd bell
Proclaims the circling hours with solemn swell—
No more the punctual tradesman marks the day;
Nor idler loiters his long hours away: .
In vain the Sun his morning beam bestows;
Here none are left to rise from night's repose:
The Moon in vain her softer radiance poürs;
None---none remain to hail the pensive hours;
Time treads his round unreckon'd and unknown;
And death-like silence claims this spot her own—
Here holds her speechless reign—here builds her mid-
　　night throne.

　　Proud e'en in ruins seems the legal hall,
Where sate the Judge rever'd and lov'd by all;
In whom unbiass'd, stubborn truth was found—
Who would be faithful—though his monarch frown'd!
True to the spirit of his country's laws,
He listen'd to no quibbles, quirks, nor flaws:
When men, demanding justice, round him drew,
The peasant and the prince no difference knew—
His smile assur'd the injur'd and opprest—
His purity proclaim'd the guiltless blest!
The felon shrank from his deep-searching look,

And with dire presage of his sentence shook!

Th' intent, and not the deed alone, he saw;

And dared bid virtue triumph over law.

No widow twice petition'd him to hear;

No friendless orphan shed a useless tear;

Nor power nor gold avail'd to screen the vile;

Or tempt his frown where duty bade him smile.

The shield of age, the monitor of youth,

His mind he lent to find the hidden truth;

Not wont to glide the surface smoothly o'er—

But doubtful subjects deeply to explore.

Mercy alone could e'er his justice move;

Slow to condemn—yet ready to approve—

His manly firmness, and his virtuous fire,

E'en those who dreaded most, would still admire.

He knew the nation on his truth relied,

To guard her peace and on her rights decide;

And thousands placed their liberties and lands,

Without one fear, in his impartial hands.

What confidence o'er all his virtue shed

What praises settled on his honour'd head

If prayers, sincerely pour'd, may blessings be—

Most blest he was—for many a prayer had he!

Peace to his ashes! he deserved the best—

His spirit long has found its heaven of rest.
How diff'rent he who oft that seat disgraced !
Thwarting the pleader with indecent haste ;
Impatient in a cause he would not like—
His eye, like angry lightnings, seem'd to strike !
In him corruption found a willing friend,
Her blackest usurpations to defend.
Opposing all improvements of the law—
His Prince's smile, the only light he saw !
Too much a courtier to be sternly just—
Too often sway'd by passion's stormy gust—
Proud, overbearing, curbing, ruling all ;
His fiat thunder'd through the startl'd hall !
Who dared a Prince's follies—crimes—to show—
Found him nor judge nor counsellor—but foe !
Toiling for infamy to blast his name,
Hated he lived, and died bereft of fame.

Beside yon churchyard wall, his wonted stand,
A sightless beggar stretch'd his needy hand :
One changeless, short petition, met the ear,
Whene'er a passing footstep sounded near—
The simple prayer—" Have pity on the blind !"
Urged its full force to every feeling mind.

Nature to him did ne'er her beauties show!
Veil'd were the clouds above, and fields below!
When morning dawn'd—he hail'd no golden ray,
Nor mark'd the crimson of the closing day:
Nor saw the beam that warm'd his cheek at noon—
Nor knew from birth the lustre of the Moon!
Shape, figure, reach'd his sense by touch alone;
And all he felt not, was to him unknown;
Veil'd was the form that brush'd him as it past,
Or in his hand the boon of pity cast;
And when the thunder roll'd its peal on high—
The lightning flash'd not on his sightless eye!
Oft have I seen some neighbour's child bestow
A welcome trifle to relieve his woe.
Wise are those parents who so soon impart
The kindliest feelings to the infant heart!
Themselves, perchance, in fortune's changing hour,
May gladden in their sympathetic power.
Fix'd to that spot, in spite of wind and rain,
Food, home, and raiment, dubious to obtain—
So past his dull, unvaried life, away,
Unchang'd by gloom of night, or blaze of day!
If that may life be call'd, that cannot mark
The morn, or eve—one midnight, long and dark—

Yes—he had night—'twas when his sorrow slept—
And morn—when from his still dark couch he crept !
All day his dog beside him stretch'd along,
Feeble in power, but in affection strong ;
In all his master's joys, though few they were,
He had an equal and a constant share ;
His wants and his commands alike he knew ;
As patient as himself—as needy too !
With more than instinct led him home at night,
Relieving by his love the loss of sight ;
His sole amusement, and his faithful guide,
He never wander'd from his master's side ;
His piteous form—his want—his tatter'd vest—
Ne'er changed th' affection of that constant breast ;
Nor would that honest brute have lov'd him more
Had gold embroider'd every garb he wore.
O ! thus denied the light of heaven to view—
What active sympathy from man is due !
Doom'd in dark listlessness to pass his days,
While manly vigour every limb displays ;
Willing to labour—but without the power—
Pity his sole dependence every hour.
But now—where does he feel his midnight way ?
Who soothes the sorrows of his sunless day ?

Perchance, e'en of his dumb conductor reft,
He finds nor home, nor hand to aid him, left;
Till, sinking, as he roams from place to place,
He dies amidst the wreck he cannot trace.

Fall'n is the mansion, where the shivering poor
Once gather'd round the hospitable door:
The home of one, by all the needy lov'd,
Whom every plaint of woe to pity mov'd:
He had a hand to raise, a heart to bless,
Whene'er he found his fellow in distress.
Though to the joys of wealth and honor born,
He never from the humble turn'd with scorn—
And, though by princes favor'd, ne'er forgot
The secret sorrows of the lowly cot:
Not like the heartless, fashionably gay,
Too proud to help the wand'rer on his way:
From ghastly want he never turn'd aside,
Nor view'd the supplicant with lordly pride.
He cheer'd the dungeon where no sunbeam shone;
Sooth'd guilt's despair, and still'd the debtor's groan;
Burst from his limbs the iron links away,
And brought him hope, and liberty, and day.
Glowing with sympathy's unfading fire,—

The widow's guardian, and the orphan's sire;
Grief would to him an equal pang impart—
A tear—th' unfailing passport to his heart!
Unostentatious of the good he did,
He, when he could, his noblest actions hid.
When evening threw her shadows on the ground,
The secret haunts of woe he sought and found;
Where many a fallen family he blest;
Too modest to solicit, though distrest!
Ah! 'tis by those, who once in sunshine dwelt,
Fate's dark'ning frown is most severely felt:
'Tis not the Prince, nor Peer, when fallen low,
Who bear the worst extremes of human woe—
A nation sympathises in their fate,
And many a wealthy friend unbars his gate—
'Tis not the vagrant and unalter'd poor,
Born in distress, and nurtur'd to endure—
As he, who lately hail'd the cheering light,
Mourns with intensest grief th' extinguish'd sight—
So they who once a competence enjoy'd,
Or in the sun of hope their powers employ'd;
Feel, when struck down to poverty and woe,
With tenfold force, the unexpected blow:
And die unseen, unaided, and alone;

Rather than make their wants and sorrows known.

When winter howl'd along the sunless air,

How many found their shelter in his care!

A mantle o'er their freezing limbs he threw;

And half disarm'd the coldest wind that blew:

Fix'd in his aim, by virtuous zeal inspir'd—

No perils check'd him, and no labours tir'd;

He brav'd the prison's pestilential breath;

And pour'd the prayer that sooth'd the pangs of death—

Though born to riches, luxury, and ease,

He past his days in scenes and toils like these;

And strove to plant in every youthful mind,

The principle of love to all mankind.

Thus, self-approving, and by thousands blest,

Sweet must have been the feelings of his breast.

So the kind Sun, by planets circl'd round,

Beams plenty, light, and joy on all around.

But now bereft of all his bounty's store,

His power to sooth and succour is no more;

Himself, perchance now wanting what he gave,

Despairing falls, without a friend to save.

Near where yon fallen column dents the ground,

A cheerful Mendicant was daily found;

A stormy life, with vigour, he had brav'd,

Till round his brow the hoary ringlets wav'd:

He counted seasons, till his hopes retir'd;

Till sons were scatter'd, and till friends expir'd:

But, though his cheeks proclaim'd the lapse of years,

Their furrows never channel'd many tears!

A well-patched wallet, swinging at his side,

A scanty meal, at Nature's call, supplied:

Upheld by confident content, he smil'd,

While passing scenes his tedious hours beguil'd;

And if of food, for present use, possest,

He trusted Providence for all the rest.

Ev'n he, at times, a generous heart could show,

And give his alms to ease another's woe!

Oft' has a group of children round him stood,

Struck with his tatter'd vest, but merry mood;

Amaz'd to see him, though so poor, so glad;

For many a tale—and many a jest he had—

The young, he said, should succour one grown grey—

The aged—him become as old as they:

Thus his request he made to all apply,

Nor e'er neglected one who past him by.

He call'd no curses on the rich who frown'd;

But like a priest shower'd blessings all around;

Blest those who, cold to pity, heard him crave ;
And doubly blest the friendly hand that gave.
What once had been a soldier's coat he wore ;
To which in shape a likeness still it bore ;
To him, it seem'd what it had earliest been—
Though scarce one thread of scarlet then was seen.
They who would stoop his varied tale to hear,
Might learn how some the ills of life can cheer ;
And find, that, in the darkest waste below,
There still are beams to gild the path of woe :
His buoyant spirit rose o'er every ill ;
And he had wit at need, and smiles at will.
Nor was it tales of mirth alone he knew—
He could talk philosophically too!
The rules and stratagems of war explain ;
And plan the field where glory pil'd the slain :
Recall the wild and desperate feats of youth;
And paint past years with more than history's truth :
Describe the scenes of many a distant clime ;
And pour a light upon the page of time.
Driv'n from this spot, where may he now appear?
Who now shall listen, and who now can cheer ?

Within yon wall I see the ruin'd pile,

Where first the rescued orphan learn'd to smile:
Where oft', at pastime's licens'd hours, the boys
Burst from confinement with exulting noise;
The task forgot, as they impell'd the ball,
Oft' seen revolving high above the wall.
Delighted have I stood to mark their sport
Within the limits of yon spacious court:
Some ran from those who watch'd their steps, to hide;
Some walk'd in life's first friendship, side by side;
Or spread the circle with united hands;
Or fought the mimic field, in hostile bands.
Ev'n they their parties form'd for love or strife—
In peace or war—a miniature of life!
Till the unwelcome bell recall'd to school,
Once more to bend to order and to rule:
Then ceased the game; each head dejected hung;
And muttering sorrow murmur'd from each tongue:
As if a sudden cloud had ris'n to shed,
O'er a bright day, a shadow deep and dread—
Till hope, that paints to every human eye,
Show'd the next hour for play, and show'd it nigh.
Tutor'd for commerce, or refin'd for art,
There emulation first inspir'd the heart,
That often with a pure, undying flame,

Impell'd them on to fortune and to fame :
While knowledge open'd to their mental eyes
Her ample stores, and bade them learn and rise.
Ill-fated boys ! here ye have play'd your last !
Here all your pleasures, all your hopes are past !
Reft by the sword from all the joys of life,
Victims of statesmen's folly—kingly strife ;
Perchance, around this ruin'd realm ye roam,
Without a tutor, and without a home,
Imploring aid—where aid is found no more—
Forgetting all that you had learn'd before—
And chang'd to vagrants, who had lived and died,
Your country's honor, and your teachers' pride.

Lone stands the Theatre, whose raptur'd crowd,
Or fix'd in silence, or applauding loud,
Beheld the mimic scene before them pass,
And look'd on life as in a magic glass—
Where man, instructed by the Poet's lays,
Compared the present with departed days ;
Where forests, caverns, mountains, met the sight—
Clothed in the blaze of day, or gloom of night :
While palaces, enchanted, seem'd to rise ;
And chambers—prisons—open'd on the eyes !

As there some vast creative power had been,
That out of nothing form'd the instant scene.
There the beholder, borne on fancy's wing,
Saw distant realms, and changing seasons spring—
Now view'd Arabia's burning desert glow;
And now the Polar waste of ice and snow—
And now the ocean, rising into wrath,
O'er which the lightning cleav'd its fiery path;
And heard the thunder rolling through the storm;
Still viewing nature in each varied form—
While, as by magic, suddenly appear—
Men, cities, of another hemisphere:
Isles where the savage lurks for human prey—
And armies marching in their long array—
Beholding, in that transient space of time,
The colour and the garb of every clime:
While the unravell'd plot held every sense
In breathless expectation, and suspense.
There the swift hours resistless laughter sped;
And many a tear at mimic woe was shed;
There poetry display'd her highest pow'rs;
And scenic fascination charm'd the hours;
While music round in sweetest echoes stole,
Rais'd the affections, and inspired the soul!

What follies have been there by wit display'd!

What scenes, what characters, from life portray'd!

Man, as he really is, unmask'd appear'd;

Admir'd, or scorn'd; detested, or rever'd.

There suff'ring virtue struggled with distress,

Yet proved at last, her power alone can bless:

While the dire passions, raging to the sight,

Taught man to shun their vortex with affright—

Anger, with swelling cheek, and looks of fire;

And dark Revenge, that fann'd her gathering ire;

And Fear, with rolling eye, and struggling breath—

And baffled Love—whose only hope was death.!

Sorrow that forc'd the genuine tear to flow;

And Jealousy that fed upon its woe—

Despair, that dar'd the last—the worst—to brave;

And Hate, that dogg'd its victim to the grave—

These, in succession, past before the view,

In all their native energy and hue!

Yes! scenes like these a generous warmth impart;

And tune to sympathy the soften'd heart:

Expand the mind—give brightness to its fire—

And love of virtue and of fame inspire;

Proud scene of art! Alas! for ever fled!

No laughter echoes, and no tears are shed:

No mimic captive groans, no hero dies,
No tyrant threatens, and no lover sighs :
Thalia 'midst the ruins walks in tears;
And in unfeign'd despair Melpomene appears.

Ye searching antiquaries ! here behold
The fate of relics, valued more than gold !
Gone are the ancient scraps that charm'd your eyes—
Stretch'd in the dust your lov'd Museum lies !
Where doubtful fragments proudly were secur'd,
If haply found in classic ground immur'd.
Coins, that scarce show'd the shadow of a head;
Or hieroglyphics, that were all but fled ;   .
And stones, with characters unknown and rude;
With transport and astonishment were view'd !
Inquiring virtuosi gather'd round,
Big with conjectures and remarks profound :
Sometimes a parchment, worn by damp or time,
A monkish legend, or a mystic rhyme—
Before them spread its almost hidden lore ;
And minds were strain'd its meaning to explore.
Some thought they saw unfolded to their view,
A field of hist'ry, and of science too ;
And hopes of fortune and of fame enjoy'd, .

That deeper search but scatter'd and destroy'd.

Their eager eyes devour'd an ancient seal;

They loved a medal better than a meal!

The feather'd kingdom rang'd the shelves along,

With all their brilliant plumes, but reft of song;

Like gaudy coxcombs, bright in outward shape,

The image of the nobler man they ape.

There stood the Lion, monarch of the plain,

And there the Tiger, who scarce own'd his reign:

Vipers, of forms repulsive, curl'd in glass,

That, arm'd with death, once lurk'd beneath the grass:

Insects, of countless species, swarm'd around;

And ocean's wrecks in inland mountains found:

And animals extinct, now turn'd to stone,

The relics of a race for ever gone:

Embalm'd by nature—coffin'd in a rock—

Preserv'd through every elemental shock;

The remnants of a former world to show,

'Ere earth's convulsions laid their species low.

The rarest, loveliest shells, from distant shores;

Metals and petrifactions, gems and ores;

The finest works of nature and of art

Were treasur'd there in one unrivall'd mart;

The bust, that sav'd from death some honor'd face;

And pictures, all but breathing life and grace :
While rude designs, from savage nations brought,
Display'd the dawn of art's awaking thought :
And manuscripts, of many an age and clime,
There rescu'd from the mould'ring touch of time,
Show'd, as they past from barbarous to refin'd,
The growth of learning, and the march of mind.
There were preserv'd the charters of the land ;
Wrung from some despot by a patriot band :
And the long, tedious toils, of letter'd men ;
And poems, dash'd from genius' fiery pen !
And there were wrecks from Egypt's ruin'd coast,
Colossal forms no later age can boast :
Whose mountain temples, and whose piles of stone
Stand in huge magnitude, unmatch'd, alone !
Whose perfect finish, and extensive plan,
Surpass the rivalship of modern man :
Works that the wrath of ages have defied ;
Performed by man in his gigantic pride :
Uniting, in their adamantine length,
His mortal science with supernal strength !
Whose sacred symbols lock'd in midnight gloom
The knowledge of the past, a letter'd tomb—
By men of learning vainly ponder'd o'er,

In hopes the marble volumes to explore :
Now clos'd from all research, in mystic night,
Unless a master key-stone spring to light.
But proudest stood the sculptor's gems of art,
Those idols worshipp'd by the wisest heart ;
And highest in the scale, fall'n Greece! were thine ;
Decreed o'er all competitors to shine :
Thou still hast left, to shame each feebler land,
The living marbles of thy matchless hand ;
Which seem to boast the immortality,
Their full, complete perfection, caught from thee!
Looking as if sense, feeling, thought, were there—
This smiling love—that shrinking in despair!
Here flashing anger ; and there frowning hate ;
As though they stood the arbiters of fate—
This, all but stepping from its pedestal—
That, as if starting back, afraid to fall !
Here smiled a Venus, rich in every grace,
That mortal form could show of limb and face ;
And there the serpents coil'd before the eye,
Till the beholder almost turn'd to fly !
These, Urburgh, were thy precious gems ; and these
Thy riches brought thee over distant seas ;
Or, in thy day of pride, by battle won,

Here shed the light of art's reviving sun :
But now in fragments strew'd by barbarous hands,
Or borne as trophied spoils to distant lands :
Passing, as power removes, from clime to clime;
Till lost for ever in the gulph of time.

Here too the sister art of Painting shone,
In all the charms peculiarly her own.
When through the long, light gallery, I pac'd,
And forms of every shape and colour trac'd ;
I seem'd to feel as on some fairy ground,
Where new creations breath'd and bloom'd around :
Where every figure fancy could divine ;
And every tint that art could lend to shine—
And every scene that genius, taste, could show;
Embodying the beautiful below—
Enchain'd the ling'ring sight, whose raptur'd sense
Alone inspir'd the soul with joy intense.
In fancy 'twas another world, that gave
To view the mighty who had past the grave—
Vision'd in thought—I seem'd myself to find
Among the greatest—brightest of mankind!
And look'd as on the living forms of men,
Whom mortal tongue could never greet again :

And held communion with the wise and just,
Whose bones for ages had been strew'd in dust!
Still—still remember'd—e'en in sorrow dear—
The shadows of those beauteous works appear;
Which here a nation's admiration drew,
And fann'd the glorious pride from whence they grew!
In memory yet full many a picture lives;
Glowing in all the fire that genius gives:
I see the forms that seem to think—to move—
Swelling in wrath—or melting into love!
The battle rages—flashes on the wall!
And armies seem to close, and squadrons fall!
Th' assassin's dagger drinks his victim's blood—
The vessel sinks beneath the whelming flood:
The ambush'd lion springs upon the steed;
Stiff'ning in fear the form he dooms to bleed!
And powers supernal glide beneath the storm,
Whom demon passions darken and deform!
The lovely landscape lengthens on the sight,
In noon's warm flush, or morning's golden light;
O'er eve's soft scene the crimson clouds are driven,
In all the varied drapery of heaven:
The distant mountains melt into the hue
That veils the horizon's verge in misty blue;

Or, pour'd upon the water, Dian's beam
Arrays in silver light the slumb'ring stream.
Th' historic scene its silent story speaks—
His hate the tyrant on the patriot wreaks !
What passions in the crowded canvass glow!
Each figure seems to act as once below—
Till the whole tale of pity, love, or ire,
Bursts on the soul in characters of fire !
And more than e'en remembrance can restore—
Here have I seen, but now can see no more.
Yet those whose treasur'd beauties still survive,
Memory in sorrow long shall keep alive ;
Long as one shadow of the past remains—
Long as the spirit drags its earthly chains.
Yet still the soul shall bless that faithful power,
That keeps some charm to sooth the present hour ;
That rescues from the past, when life was bright,
Some form to cheer its dim succeeding night ;
And gives the spirit, else of all bereft,
The only beam a darken'd fate has left.
So the worn traveller, fix'd at home at last,
Reviews the brightest scenes through which he past ;
And thither borne on fancy's wing of light,
Ponders their beauties with renew'd delight.

Far different scene did yon recess display—
Where, veil'd in clouds of smoke that darken'd day,
A crowded, noisy Manufactory stood ;
A source of public or of private good.
There did a toiling race their lives employ,
And thence arose each dearly purchas'd joy :
The long—long hours, in changeless dullness, past ;
Each day, each year, a picture of the last—
The drear, uninteresting task, the same ;
Life, scarce relieved by pleasure, hope, or fame.
There did they hasten soon as morning rose ;
And there were chain'd beyond the evening's close :
From earliest youth the beaten path they trod ;
Nor left it—but to mingle with the sod.
For them the sweets of nature bloom'd in vain :
The scented valley, and the breezy plain ;
Scarce for their eyes the golden clouds appear'd—
Nor for their feet the hills their summits rear'd—
Scarce time could father spare t'embrace his child—
Few days of joy a darken'd year beguil'd ;
'Twas toil—'twas sleep—a hurried meal—a breath ;
A cold, dark, caged existence, closed by death ;
There droop'd the fetter'd soul ; the gifted mind,

Sunk to the lowest level of its kind ;

And feeling that her wings could never soar,

Her pinions clos'd, and thought of flight no more !

O ! surely, bounteous Heav'n could ne'er decree

Such gloom should shroud the spirit's brilliancy:

Did never that ethereal light bestow

To die in darkness, or to set in woe'!

The glorious hand that plac'd the Sun on high,

Gave it to glow—to shine—for every eye :

No niggard of his boon, he shower'd on earth

Blessings for all, the right of all by birth ;

Nor e'er intended that incessant toil

Should freeze the heart's last hope, the lip's last smile.

And truth proclaims that land's unnatural state,

Where half the people sink in wayward fate ;

Who sleep to dream of joy that ne'er arrives ;

And only wake to labour through their lives :.

Where noary age is torn from rest away,

And fetter'd childhood weeps its loss of play ;

And manhood sees his years of prime expire,

As the Sun wastes on desert sands his fire.

The state's demands, each year increasing, tore

From the despairing labourers half their store ;

And left them in their ravag'd homes to feel
The desolating wounds they could not heal!
Now freed too late, perchance the hostile change
But leaves them houseless wanderers to range.

THE

DESERTED CITY.

PART II.

Scenes of all hues, and life in every form,
The dark, the bright, the frozen, and the warm—
Urburgh, within thy ample space were seen—
Revel and want—and but a wall between!
Here wild profusion—naked famine there—
Here care unknown—there nothing left but care!
Behind where some proud mansion rear'd its head—
Cold winds pierc'd poverty's unfurnish'd shed:
Close by some glitt'ring dome, where all was bright,
Lay sorrow shrouded in unbroken night:
The very stones where want dropt down to die,
Shook with the equipage that rattled by;
Whose passing torches' ostentatious glare

Flash'd on the houseless victim of despair!

Here burst the long-loud laugh—there heav'd the
    groan—

Circl'd by anguish—pleasure fix'd her throne!

Show'ring on those who throng'd her golden seat,

For each enraptur'd sense, allurements sweet—

Shedding abundant on the crowded board

The best that art could yield, or earth afford;

And mingling with the wealth of every clime,

Whate'er amusement could give wings to time—

The play; the masquerade at midnight hour;

The concert, fraught with soul inspiring power;

The witching dance that bids an evening fly,

Swift as the convict's who is soon to die:

Where beauty trod with sylph-like step its maze;

And seem'd to grow still lovelier to the gaze:

The scenes where luxury and wealth combin'd

To banish sorrow, and enchant the mind:

Where sparkling chandeliers, with starry light,

Shone out triumphant o'er the reign of night;

While art and nature seem'd in contest there,

To deck the noble, and adorn the fair!

The crimson ruby, and the sapphire blue,

Glitter'd with every motion on the view:

The sunny diamond sparkled on the sight,

And flash'd its dazzling tints upon the night.

There man assumed his fair, but specious form,

Frigid, tho' bright, as ice-drops in the storm;

With elegance of manners, wit, and ease,

Devoting life in learning but to please ;

With smiling magic winding round the heart;

Blinding the thoughtless to the veil of art;

Whose soul, with more than iron mask conceal'd,

One real thought or feeling scarce reveal'd.

Young beauty there, (whose loveliest tint is still

The blush that neither comes nor goes at will,

But passes like the crimson cloud at eve,

That seems on earth a softer bloom to leave—)

Met the full gaze of crowds in conscious pride,

Nor shrank within herself, nor turn'd aside;

But knew the bold, repelling glance, to throw

On those she did not court, or would not know!

Cold, empty Fashion! heartless is thy form!

No love can thrill it, and no friendship warm :

Each genuine feeling of the soul by thee ,

Is check'd, or withers in thy lethargy;

Wavering as meteors in the northern sky,

No useful beam thou shed'st on heart nor eye ;

D

To scenes that might the feeling soul inspire
Thy vacant look denies one spark of fire:
Oft' have I seen thee, when the Tragic Muse
Essay'd her melting influence to diffuse;
Gaze on the anguish'd, or terrific scene,
With tranquil eye, and cold, unalter'd mien;
While other cheeks were glistening with the tear,
And other breasts were harrow'd up with fear:
Sense, genius, passion, weigh'd against thy power,
Nor rouse the mind, nor rule one tender hour.
Ah! happier far, the scene of friends belov'd!
Congenial souls, long known, and often prov'd:
Where the full tide of feeling pours its stream,
And the heart gladdens in the eyes' bright beam;
Where all the treasur'd stores of mind are brought
T'enrich the feast of fancy and of thought—
Where tho' wit strike, mirth draws its barb away;
And heart-born smiles on sunny features play.
In such a scene how swift the moments sped!
The night was ended ere the charm had fled!
So while we gaze eve's gorgeous clouds to mark,
Ere we can trace their forms the heavens are dark:
Too soon dispersed, like those we lov'd to greet,
Till desolation circles round our feet;

And silent darkness fills the place which they
Peopled and brighten'd in life's younger day.
With them we snatch the golden hours of life—
The rest are passion, storm, disgust, or strife:
Then only shine the rays that burst between
The clouds of fate, to cheer life's checquer'd scene—
Save to the few, whose souls of wilder mood,
Find rapture in the depths of solitude;
Companion'd by each vast and thrilling thought,
And beings in the womb of fancy wrought;
Whose minds create what earth nor heaven has known,
Who scarce remember that they breathe alone.

In yon raz'd College, youth shall learn no more;
Nor doctors dully doze o'er classic lore;
Nor history her mould'ring page unroll;
Nor science raise on high th' expanding soul:
Nor gifted boys, to emulation fired,
Pant to be heard, and envied, and admired!
There every study that could lift the thought,
Before the deep and ardent mind was brought.
That proudly started from its brighter birth;
And soar'd on high, and spurn'd the bounds of earth;
And mark'd, in the unmeasured realms of light,

The planet's circle, and the comet's flight;
Traced suns on suns, that, 'midst the starry spheres,
Bestow'd on countless worlds their days and years.
While nature's mystic laws, unknown before,
Their powers reveal'd, and work'd unknown no more.
The mind its faculties distinguish'd, trac'd;
In judgment strengthen'd, and refin'd in taste.
There the young Poet burn'd the prize to win—
Bade ardent fancy's soaring flight begin;
And fann'd the spark of that etherial fire,
That beam'd a Sun for nations to admire.
But there no more the tutor'd soul shall rise,
Panting to mingle with her native skies.
Within those walls the monumental bust
Rescued the form that time had strew'd in dust;
Where, chisell'd on the long enduring stone,
The features of departed genius shone—
Reft—crush'd by havoc's desolating sweep—
Now scarce a marble marks the great who sleep;
And all that fate has left the living—is to weep!

No more beside the hero's trophied urn,
The fearless soldier feels his bosom burn;
Reviews the past in admiration dumb—

Or fondly pictures triumphs yet to come!
Nor near the Poet's tomb the friend of art
Feels inspiration kindling at his heart!
But ah! how many of that fated race
Have left their bones where nothing marks the place;
Save the wild-flower that blooms above their head,
And drops the only tear that's o'er them shed.
Often, like meteors shooting thro' the night,
They lighten on the world—and sink from sight!
Too oft', like spirits of another sphere,
Wand'ring, they find no kindred beings here—
Strangers amidst the crowd they battle through—
Absorbed in fancy's intellectual view—
Scorning and scorn'd by traffic's sordid crew;
They breathe—they move—as if they liv'd alone;
Or in a wild creation of their own!
Scarce of the earth that bears their alien tread;
They live in storms, and tempests wrap their head:
With thoughts, and hopes, and feelings, none can
    share—
They start away and perish in despair.

Here oft' I gazed, while, slowly passing by,
The long procession proudly caught the eye;

In military pomp, or civic pride,
And lin'd with armed hosts on either side;
Whether it grac'd some warrior's funeral hour,
Or led the monarch in his pride of power;
With statesmen, heroes, princes in the train—
And graced with all wealth, valor, could obtain!
Such myriads throng'd, as if the nation there,
Came with one mind the grief or joy to share.
If chance some victory had plum'd the land,
Exulting thousands pour'd along the strand;
And while the cannon roll'd the news around,
Each seem'd to triumph in the welcome sound.
The joyous lamps dispell'd the shades of night;
Arranged like stars, with every colour bright;
Or Iris' bow revers'd in many-tinted light:
Aloft, transparent, painted trophies hung,
And with the conqueror's name the city rung!
All left their homes the midnight joy to share!
And with proud acclamations rent the air.
Alas! they thought not then how dearly bought
Those triumphs, and how soon to turn to nought:
They did not deem that fame, so vainly won,
Would leave their country beggar'd and undone.
Alas! the pomp no more shall traverse here!

And victory's last shout hath left the ear!
O'er all, a silent melancholy reigns,
That spreads (contagious) to the neighbouring plains.

Alone I pace thro' traffic's busiest seat,
Where thousands lately throng'd the noisy street;
Where beauty loiter'd many a vacant morn,
Seeking whatever might her charms adorn;
Convinced that dress imparts a higher grace
To each perfection of the form and face.
And men (tho' few) more frivolous than they,
Here traced the changing fashions of the day;
Whose dearth of mind, or idleness of thought—
'Twas all they could—that poor distinction sought!
To glitter like the gaudy butterfly—
To live—be seen—to flutter—and to die!
Here form'd for pride, or luxury, or use,
Was found whate'er art, nature, could produce:
Now the bright mantle caught th' admiring gaze—
Now gold and jewels shed their mingled rays:
And all the lures of trade, and powers of art,
Seem'd centred in one great capacious mart.
The few, by learning led, by genius fired,
To nobler fame, and loftier thoughts aspired:

Rapt in philosophy's sublimest height,

Or in the Poets' wild.etherial flight,

Eager each maze of science to explore,

Ambitious to increase their mental store—

They, 'midst the letter'd treasures, lov'd to seek

The volumes where the great departed speak;

Or living writers vied with Roman and with Greek.

And here the glass, defying space, was made,

To show the heavens in all their pride display'd;

Whose lengthen'd vision brings the planet nigh,

That shoots no ray to man's unaided eye,

Lost with its moons amidst the boundless sky—

Nor less amazing, that which brings to light

Myriads of forms, impalpable to sight;

But which, beneath the optic power, appear

An almost hidden world of beings here;

Active with life as those that tread the plain—

Perchance as sensible of joy or pain!

Perfect in parts, a countless, varied race;

With scarce a portion of the realm of space!

Thus shown, the insect we might crush unseen,

A bulk gigantic wears, and monster's mien!

And here th' electric tube reveal'd to sight

The mystic fluid of supernal might:

Whose dread explosion rends the echoing air,
As if unearthly beings battled there;
While midnight lightning frights the timid soul;
And lengthen'd peals of thunder shake the pole!
The painted globe display'd its varied book,
For man to look on, as a God might look—
Who sees the earth an atom whirling round—
A speck amidst the infinite profound!
Yet, on its narrow space, what passions burn,
Blight its fair face, and man to demon turn.
Upon some plain he casts his craving eye—
There slays his kind—and then lies down to die!
Whate'er could vigour to his mind impart,
Or prove the depth of thought, the powers of art;
All that could splendour on his days bestow—
Here perfect shone—the noon of life below.

Scarce can I trace where once the Tavern stood,
Where men of learning met in cheerful mood;
Where oft', when twilight robed the west in gray,
They came to close in joy a studious day:
Then various questions bred debates profound,
Broken as wine or wit by turns went round!
There Philo boasted how he knew the men

Who ruled the realm—what they design'd, and when—
What letter last he penn'd to save the state—
What satire levell'd at the guilty great!
The Poet there reveal'd his patron's name,
His fancied guide to fortune and to fame!
To doubtful friends his sanguine hopes display'd;
And had been happy—had his debts been paid.
The Critic told—as much as critics do—
What pages then were passing in review:
What wings were clipt, to check the further flight
Of some young bard, who aim'd to reach the height
Parnassus tempting shows—what work struck dead,
Left harmless curses on his nameless head.
The Doctor there forgot his numerous slain,
Laugh'd o'er the glass, and ' was himself again'!
And men of letters show'd some rare unique,
Purchas'd, perchance, where none such gem would seek.
Lov'd scene of converse! seat of mental glee!
Now lost for ever both to them and me!
Where such a circle can I hope to find?
Such letter'd friendship, or such feast of mind?
Each intellectual joy has taken flight,
And learning finds another Gothic night:
Refinement backward treads her steps again,

And man has toil'd a thousand years in vain!
So when an earthquake shakes a polish'd realm,
And the ground opens, cities, plains, to whelm;
A wild and barren desert meets the day;
Whence all the pride of art has sunk away.

Near where yon obelisk its point displays,
A Market echo'd on accustom'd days;
Whose numerous lights, upon the evening air,
Shed far around a red and wavering glare:
Where, jostling through the crowd, and viewing all,
The laborer urg'd his way from stall to stall.
There did the sun-burnt gardener weekly bring
The fruits of autumn, or the flowers of spring;
And many a farmer thither brought his store,
Who having sold it, car'd for nothing more.
There half the neighbouring fields their treasures pour'd;
And plenty seem'd to spread the general board;
Earth, ocean, air, their various tribes supplied—
For man's repast, fish, fowl, and flock had died!
Who there might gaze, would never dream of dearth;
It seem'd the very magazine of earth!
While rattling bustle and tumultuous noise,
Echoed from wheels and horses, men and boys;

Superior far, though grating to the ear,
Than the dead silence now prevailing here.

Fall'n—desert City! splendid was thy state!
Ages had o'er thee roll'd to make thee great!
Tempest and toil thy people struggled through,
To see thee rise in grandeur to the view!
How slowly did thy temples pierce the day!
How gradually thy streets their length display:
Year after year beheld them stretch along;
And peopled by a still increasing throng—
With ceaseless step they pierc'd the fields around,
Till mansions prest the lately cultur'd ground;
And roof and steeple glitter'd in the sky,
Where recent woods had waved their boughs on high!
Nought stopt thy progress! forest—river—hill—
Beheld thee pass their feeble barriers still—
O'er leafless leagues one mass of buildings spread;
Till every trace of rural life had fled!
Till e'en the villages that round thee bloom'd,
At last within thy giant grasp were tomb'd.
It seem'd as if mankind had gather'd there,
One general fate of good or ill to share:
The foot that tried to trace thy ample round,

Wearied ere half thy devious course was found.
The wond'ring traveller hail'd thy noontide fame,
And the whole world resounded with thy name.
But ah! how quickly in destruction strew'd,
When fled thy people, scatter'd and subdued!
Thus the slow oak expands in pride below—
But struck by lightning, withers at a blow!
As scenes of past prosperity appear,
Who now could view thee and refuse the tear?
'Midst the drear shadows of this wreck I trace
The banish'd pleasures of each well known place—
Till darker grow the ruins on mine eye,
And grief compels the unavailing sigh.

Pass we this gate, beneath the colonnade;
The pillars in the square within display'd,
Enclose the area of the late Exchange;
Where captains, merchants, mingled to arrange
The world's vast trade, as though all nations there,
Came its enriching intercourse to share.
Men from all climes, as if by one consent,
Met in one throng, inspir'd by one intent;
From Europe's nearest and remotest shore—
And Western Islands where tornadoes roar—

From Asia's groves, once man's fair seat of prime;
And Afric, hindmost in the march of time—
. From wide Columbia, bursting into power,
Where freedom fled in her despairing hour;
When, of each famed and cherish'd spot bereft,
She sought the sole asylum fate had left;
'Till renovating time should call her back,
To bless once more each early favor'd track.
Of all the world this spot might seem the heart:
That urged the vital stream to every part:
Whence each to others sent what each could spare,
Till nature's bounty all contrived to share!
The rich abundance of the fruitful field—
What surplus stores the hand of toil could yield—
Here found a ready mart, a transfer sure,
To bless the wealthy, and enrich the poor.
Here rival nations, spite of hate or pride,
Seem'd in one social brotherhood allied;
As if war, interest, ne'er had spread a cloud,
The sunshine of so fair a scene to shroud.

And near that busy spot the Bank arose;
The nation's pride—the envy of her foes!
Whence, as from some exhaustless mine of gold,

The stream of wealth o'er all the country roll'd;

And distant realms, and hostile too, had share

In riches' magic influence reigning there:

As there had work'd some deep pervading spell,

That drew from every clime its stores to swell;

And bade all earth in confidence repose

On honor that was sacred e'en to foes.

And thence the vital stream return'd to all,

Like welcome showers on burning fields that fall;

Or some unfailing spring that bursts to light,

And onward rolls increasing to the sight:

Till o'er the land the fruitful river pours,

And loads with riches its exulting shores;

Then mingles with the sea, and spreads around,

Wherever ocean rolls, or man is found.

What joyous crowds each day collected there,

The produce of their treasur'd hoards to share!

How many thousands drew from thence th' increase

That blest their days with ease, their nights with peace!

The spring of commerce, and the heart of trade,

It bade its influence all the land pervade;

And if the sudden cry of war arose—

It arm'd the hosts that flew to meet their foes;

And launch'd the fleets that swept the vanquish'd
   main,
The nation's glory foremost to maintain !
The bulwark of the land—the soul of all—
Its honour stood unquestion'd in its fall !
And when it fell, in hostile ruin hurl'd—
It seem'd as if an earthquake shook the world !
And distant cities started from their sleep ;
And nations woke to hear the tale and weep ;
And lamentations rose from every shore,
That one so rich—so mighty—was no more !

Ill-fated land ! to ruin doom'd a prey !
Where wars perpetual sweep mankind away !
Or whence the riches of the nation fly,
That distant lands may mourn, and armies die.
In vain thy fields with rip'ning treasures bloom—
Amidst their wealth want oft' but finds a tomb !
In vain thy merchants and thy peasants toil,
While war exhausts thee, or while armies spoil !
False is the smile that decks thy laborer's cheek—
And ill conceals the dread he fears to speak !
And still the mask of safety covers all—

Nor drops—but at the nation's final fall.

Even when subjugation hovers nigh,

The gilded surface cheats the patriot eye :

And though each ruler knows his country's state—

And every peasant trembles for her fate—

Still will th' infatuate statesmen of the land,

Provoke the vengeance of a hostile hand ;

Or goad her, till impatient of the chain,

She rise to burst the galling links in twain.

In such a realm—O ! what must man endure!

No joy is certain, and no life secure.

From such a land—the seat of strife and woe ;

In search of happier climes, the people go.

But much, and long—(though scarce in hope,)they bear ;

Ere from their father's graves their steps they tear—

Ere from the seat of youth's past joys they fly,

Upon some foreign, friendless shore, to die !

A thousand strong attachments rise around,

To chain their footsteps to that hallow'd ground :

Still dear to sight their childhood scenes appear ;

And in the parting moment—doubly dear!

The barren heath that infant footsteps prest,

May breathe enchantment round the manly breast;

The stream where boyhood plunged his limbs to lave,

In age's eye seems an unalter'd wave—

The trees—the rocks—that rise in native air;

This mystic—nameless sense—appear to share!

The links of friendship—kindred's heartstring ties—

That bind the spirit to its native skies—

And all those feelings tongue can scarce define,

Home's magic charms around the soul entwine—

These may be·felt, but scarcely can be told;

Nor oft are sever'd till the breast is cold.

Yet fate, despite of all these bonds, may tear

The soul away; wrongs, sorrows, none can bear,

May urge the man some kinder spot to find,

Who leaves his fondest feelings still behind.

But oh! what wrongs, what sorrows must they be,

To launch him thus on fortune's treacherous sea;

When habits, fix'd like instinct in the soul,

Have power each thought and feeling to controul—

Commencing life anew, when cares should cease;

And labor rest upon the lap of peace;

Where scarce a hope can rise, ere life must close,

To see the dawn of pleasure, or repose.

They whose misrule compels such hearts to roam,

Should live to feel how keen the loss of home;

To sigh their last beneath some distant skies,
And sink, without a friend to close their eyes.
Yes! spite of all these spells of soul, they flee—
'Tis their sole hope—some land more just to see!
Where peace may still her calm assurance spread,
And equal laws their guarding influence shed:
Where night in safe repose may steal away,
Contentment bless, and hope illume the day:
Where dying they may trust their sons will see
Life growing—bright'ning in prosperity;
And where at least the fruits of toil will yield
Their boon to him who cultivates the field.
The merchant takes his wealth to climes like these,
There to ensure tranquillity and ease;
The swain seeks ground secure from hostile tread,
Content to find some peace-protected shed:
Blest that his toil may not be spent in vain
For hearts that spurn him—hands that forge his chain.
Urg'd by distress, the sons of art retire,
Where hope may cheer them, and success inspire;
They quit a land with pomp, not freedom, graced;
A noble desert, and a splendid waste!
Far—far they urge their distant course away,
Through wat'ry wastes to realms of brighter day:

A rising nation hails them to her shore,

And bids the welcome wand'rers fear no more!

Such emigrations feed a new-born state,

But urge the realm they quit to swifter fate;

The heart's best blood forsakes the fated land;

Its absent treasures aid that rival's hand:

Th' unlessen'd burthens those they leave must bear,

Until taxation battles with despair!

The handicraftsmen there their arts pursue,

And prove a source of power, and riches too.

Thus rolls the ceaseless change from shore to shore—

Thus nations rise—thus fall to rise no more!

The seat of empire moves from clime to clime,

Nor e'er prevails against the power of time.

So here the ocean gains upon the land—

And there, receding, leaves a blooming strand;

Till over spire and turret rolls the wave,

Or cities rise upon the coral cave!

Urburgh o'er every realm her flag unfurl'd;

Herself an island—yet she awed the world!

When she arose, and bared her mighty arm

For battle—nations trembled with alarm—

Her look was lightning—and a thunder peal

Her threat; that made the hostile shores to reel.

Her giant grasp embraced from pole to pole;
And east and west own'd her supreme controul:
Men of all tongues, all climes, confess'd her reign,
Queen of the isles, and mistress of the main.
But, like a brilliant star that bursts to sight,
Her empire spread in wreck, and sank in night.
Yet still—her name—her glory, ne'er can die,
While earth shall track her orbit through the sky.
'Tis true, the greatest states decline and fall;
But to their rulers we impute it all.
Look back! and trace, in the historic scene,
What Carthage, Rome, and more as proud have been—
Then say what strew'd their honors in the dust,
But wasting wars, and governments unjust!
It is not that th' exhausted earth denies
The seed to ripen—'tis not that the skies
Refuse to bless her with the timely shower;
Nor is it that the sun withholds his power—
The ground is fertile still; the seasons roll;
And summer, winter, pass o'er either pole:
The morn yet rises on his golden wing,
And evening falls her balmy dews to fling—
Still nature pours her wealth o'er hill and plain;
'Tis man alone that makes her bloom in vain.

Yes—life has evils! earth is charged with woe!
Unclouded fortune ne'er was found below!
Here warring passions strew the wreck of strife—
There nature rends with pain the strings of life!
The flowery prospects of the youthful eye
A darken'd scene in manhood's vigour die;
And manhood's hopes—since hope can scarce be
    lost—
Set in the lasting chill of age's frost!
Oft' by Volcanoes realms in wreck are hurl'd;
A sacrifice, perchance, to save a world—
Yet Nature's general laws are more than kind;
Man is the greatest foe that man can find.
If Nature rend the earth—she heals the wound!
To hide the ruin—spreads profusion round!
Man leaves the victim who has met his blow,
'Till the last drop, unstaunch'd, unwept, shall flow!
Whether she smite with fire, or flood, or air,
Nature but seldom leaves complete despair;
But the dark ruin of despotic sway
Blasts earth and man, and sweeps his hopes away.
Eats, like the Mole, the germ of future wealth;
And poisons all the springs of life and health:
Steals the sole joy the sinking poor have left;

Whose last is gone when liberty is reft.

Thou, Urburgh! of this curse hadst more than share—

A century saw thee verging to despair!

Slowly but sure the secret poison work'd—

Deep in thy heart its deadly influence lurk'd—

Long years of wasteful war thy vitals wore;

And pour'd thy gold on many a hostile shore;

Till burthens destin'd for a race unborn,

Made thee of earth the beacon and the scorn.

Thou who unharm'd—untouch'd—might'st still have
    stood—

To aid the cause of despots shed thy blood!

Who having triumph'd, leagu'd to bind in chains

The cheated world, and robb'd thee for thy pains.

Thy rulers, selfish, cruel, and unjust,

Devour'd thy wealth, and strew'd thy rights in dust:

Too often ranged against the public weal,

With scarcely souls to judge, or hearts to feel;

Clinging to power, despite of public hate;

Urging with desperate acts the nation's fate—

Blind to the mental progress of mankind;

Themselves the hindmost in the march of mind;

In them nor art nor science found a friend,

One cheering smile, one aiding hand to lend;

In their despite improvements spread along,
Till mightiest spirits started from the throng ;
And bay'd them to their teeth, and dar'd their power ;
And shook the throne itself in that wild hour !
Once, from all climes, men flew to thee for aid—
Then—thy rich left thee, lonely and betray'd !
Thy noblest spirits sought some happier realm,
Ere all their hopes thy hast'ning fate should whelm ;
Or too indignant to endure the chain,
They saw thee, heaving, pant to burst in vain.
Each class sank slowly in the social scale ;
Th' industrious found their toil of no avail ;
And famine, stealing to the laborer's cot,
Breathed life's last curse on his unhappy lot.
When want in threat'ning murmurs found a vent—
Then—did the tyrants tremble and relent ?
No ! despots for themselves alone can feel—
They heard the prayer—they answer'd with the steel !
They first embrued the sword in native blood ;
That pour'd in after times a hideous flood :
That sword, they deem'd, would still a nation's cries ;
And silence wrongs that thunder'd to the skies.
Weak—shallow hope ! when men have reach'd the
    worst,

Their wrath explodes in one volcanic burst!
'Tis not for him to fear the chance of strife,
Who finds no blessing left to sweeten life —
Assured no change—whatever change may be—
Can see him deeper sunk in misery.
And who, with mortal feelings, fails to chuse
The chance to win, with nothing left to lose?
On whom, should death alight, it does but shed
The long repose that stills the aching head.
'Twas then, when civil strife the land assail'd,
The watchful foe attack'd her and prevail'd :
'Twas then the ruin, such as now I see,
Fell on my hapless country, and on me.

Yes! I remember well that fatal day
When noble Urburgh fell, the despots' prey :
The previous night, when hostile armies closed
Around her barriers, not an eye reposed ;
Thousands were listening to the distant drum,
To judge how nigh the gathering foe was come :
The cannons' bursting sound, that cleav'd the air,
Was follow'd by the blankness of despair!
At intervals some shooting rocket rose,
A signal to direct the march of foes.

E

The mansions pour'd their inmates on the street,
Where mingling strangers seem'd like friends to meet;
At every turn some crowd consulting stood,
Dreading the coming morn would rise in blood.
And there was hurrying, rushing to and fro
Of man and horse—a people whelm'd in woe!
And men were shouting for their friends; and cries
Of women trembled in the echoing skies!
The high—the low—were blended in one throng,
That like a stormy river roll'd along;
All ranks abroad, as by one impulse, flock'd,
Leaving their dwellings darken'd and unlock'd;
Save where a light through some lone casement beam'd,
That like a meteor o'er the tempest gleam'd;
Whose inmates hurried through the sleepless night
The preparation for the morrow's flight.
The time had been—and here—when such an hour
Had found those thousands sunk in slumber's power—
Breathing unconscious life, or dreaming bliss—
But sleep could never reign o'er scene like this;
Where shouts and curses—terror and despair—
Roll'd all their mingled sounds along the air.
Once he who through the streets, at midnight, past,
Might deem himself of all mankind the last;

So peaceful, solitary, still and dead—
As all who throng'd them yesterday were fled—
Now—'twas but like a day bereft of light;
A sunless noon of tempest and affright!

Thousands departed ere the morning rose,
That saw the City traversed by her foes:
'Twas the last day that shone upon her fame—
The evening left her nothing but a name—
That now resounds a warning word to all,
Of the sure causes of a nation's fall.
Who lived of her enslavers, fled the first—
The hopeless—reckless—stay'd to brave the worst!
In sullen hate upon the foe they gazed;
And cursed the hostile flag that triumph raised;
Borne by the very hands that oft' before
Had lost the trophies Urburgh proudly wore.
In endless columns they advanc'd along,
Safe in her weakness, and in numbers strong;
Like the fierce torrent that the mountain pours,
Tearing the ravaged vales through which it roars.
The heavy tread of many thousand feet,
Shaking the ground, past on from street to street;
The tramp of steed follow'd the rumbling gun,

And noon was glowing ere their march was done.
The drums that peal'd their thunder on the air,
Roll'd the last echoes of a land's despair;
And the shrill trumpet's loud and piercing breath,
Burst on the fallen like the blast of death!
Yes—there were bitter feelings none could speak—
And proud men look'd the wrath they could not wreak—
And they whose hopes had with their country's grown,
Long'd for a look might turn that host to stone!
The pride of manhood struggled with despair;
And hands were clench'd as if a sword were there;
And the last feeling of the soul was shame,
That thus should set their country's star of fame.

Collected in one Square, a patriot band,
Held life's last struggle for their native land;
Who rather than behold her final woe,
Would fight to save, or fall amidst the foe.
How fierce—how fatal—in that spot, the strife!
None would surrender—though the boon was life!
From every street that form'd an entrance there,
The foe advanced to wedge them in despair:
From every opening rending thunders pour'd,
That, echoing round, in long loud vollies roar'd:

Through living lines of men the bolts were hurl'd,
Which, as they heard them, dash'd them from the world.
That post they held ev'n while they shed their blood ;
Slaughter'd and crush'd in masses as they stood :
The dead and mangled that around them lay,
A rampart seem'd to keep the foe at bay ;
Where muskets rested on some friend's cold form,
Prolong'd the fierce, but unavailing storm.
The iron shower in fatal fury flew—
The strife of wrath more wild and deadly grew ;
As the long rumbling tempest pours at last
Its deepest rage in one collected blast !
Oft' fell some shatter'd building's loosen'd wall,
That whelm'd the dead and living in its fall—
Oft' the foe rush'd into the charnel square—
As oft' retiring, left their bravest there !
Still the last wreck of that determin'd band
Braced every nerve to perish hand to hand !
Then close they came, and vengeance had her fill,
And life's last energies were rous'd to kill :
And the hot breath was felt, (so near they drew—)
As if the purple blast of poison blew.
There scarce was room to whirl the sword around,
That rose to cleave its victim to the ground :

While grappling, even in the pangs of death,
They look'd the curse that fell with life's last breath.
From house to house they fought—from room to room,
And in those lordly mansions met their doom :
Doors shatter'd—stain'd with blood—remain'd to tell
The tale of those who bravely fought and fell :
And heroes dropp'd, life's crimson stream to pour
Upon the richly decorated floor ;
And shouts and tumults in those chambers rung,
Where night her veil o'er silent couches flung :
Where once the concert pour'd its witching strain,
Echoed the clash of swords, the groans of pain !
Floors, where the joyous dance its mazes spread,
Shook with the struggling warriors' heavy tread :
Where elegance in golden luxury dwelt—
Where every bliss of polish'd life was felt—
The rage of slaughter breathed—the blows of death
    were dealt !
So oft' some sweetly smiling, favor'd scene,
Adorn'd with flowers, and ever cloth'd in green ;
Where ages past had smoothly roll'd away ;
Nor brought one freezing, burning, stormy day—
Beholds at last a sudden tempest driven,
Gather'd and borne upon the winds of heaven ;

That bursts with desolating force around,
And strews with wreck the lately smiling ground.

The day's last streak of light dissolved away;
The strife was done—for none were left to slay!
Of all that desperate, devoted band,
Not one remain'd to move a hostile hand.
Their patriot fire was quench'd—their duty o'er—
The spark extinct that nothing can restore!
And they were stretch'd upon the silent bier;
The last—sole resting place, that waits us here.
Though late so anxious—then it wrung them not
Though war their nation from the earth should blot—
They died attempting to maintain her blest,
Nor foe nor tyrant more could mar their rest.
Their grave—that ground on which their faith they prov'd,
Was still their portion in the land they lov'd.

But how felt they—whose lot had there been cast
In peace and hope—now hope was almost past!
Who saw in horror, stupor, or despair,
The storm of war let loose in fury there!
There—where their mornings broke in tranquil light;
And fear ne'er stole upon the stilly night:

Who view'd their homes, the prey of lawless bands;
Their mansions kindled by enfuriate hands,
Their own, and children's heritage, destroy'd;
Their native scenes a wreck'd and blacken'd void!
That night—who saw it, and has being yet,
Its blasting horrors never can forget!
The plund'ring foe swept the vast city round,
And made a spoil of all the wealth they found:
And many a cry, from victims in their power,
Pierc'd through the roar of that tumultuous hour!
But some, who straggled from their host too far,
Flash'd their last glance upon the midnight star;
Vengeance assail'd them where was no retreat,
And patriot weapons slew them in the street;
So vast the circuit of the city spread,
Thousands might fall, and pile the heap of dead;
Nor distant friends the shout of tumult hear;
Nor scarce the cannon's signal reach the ear:
In suburbs far remote, resistance rose;
And bath'd their pavements in the blood of foes.
One man I knew—and he was desperate then—
In happier times the best of patriot men;
Alone his house he paced, resolved to die,
If o'er his threshold past an enemy:

The warlike powder lay in heaps below;
And torch, hand, heart—were ready for the blow!
Determin'd with one blast to dash away
Himself, and them, ere he would fall their prey!
The foe beheld—and shudder'd at the sight,
And left him to his desolated right.
Some silent, reckless, in their chambers sate;
Nor sought, nor shunn'd, nor scarcely fear'd their
    fate.
Gaz'd on the flame's red glow, that spread on high;
And listen'd to the shouts that rent the sky;
With all that apathy the wretch may know,
Who counts the number of his hours below;
While those who still thought being worth their care,
Fled from the wreck in terror and despair;
Though strong affections, that still clung behind,
With keenest anguish wrung the tortur'd mind.
Forc'd from their homes, from scenes so long ador'd,
From every avenue their numbers pour'd;
The man of wealth, and luxury, and pride,
Disdain'd not, in the flight, the beggar's side;
Th' industrious artizan, in deep despair,
Lost all the savings of a life of care;
His wife, in fear and sorrow, grasp'd his arm;

Her sole defence against impending harm :
In love's strong clasp his trembling child he prest,
And felt its beating heart against his breast;
More dearly priz'd, as danger drew more nigh,
Determin'd to preserve it, or to die!
The tradesman fled his venerated home;
A wand'rer in the eve of life to roam :
And females, madden'd by the worst of fears,
Their hearts in anguish, and their eyes in tears;
Nurtur'd in scenes of elegance and ease;
Grac'd by each polish'd art, and form'd to please—
Then did their delicate and lovely forms
Endure, unhous'd, the rudely beating storms.
Youths with fond care their feeble parents led ;
And dried with filial love the tears they shed :
Some silent droop'd, as in life's last despair—
Others with fruitless cries assail'd the air.
Still, as with heavy heart the gate they past,
One feeling bade them turn and look their last!
Weeping the ruin that they could not stem,
They fled what had been all the world to them :
Danger behind them, and distress before ;
E'en hope portray'd not one bright scene in store.
And O! if there be aught the mind can wring;

Or plant in life's last days a cureless sting;
'Tis to be doom'd in age from home to part,
And force to unknown scenes a wither'd heart—
To feel affections, habits, wrench'd away—
And yet find all these griefs too weak to slay;
Backward to turn in vain the longing eye,
Yet farther stray beneath an alien sky;
To wake, when life hath lost its wish to range,
To new disquiets and a hopeless change.

Accursed War! thou foe of ev'ry joy!
Thou dost but move creation to destroy!
The plains are blacken'd by thy fiery path;
And blooming valleys wither in thy wrath:
There blazing cities turn th' horizon red—
And here the ashes of a village spread!
Shedding on man and earth thy pois'nous breath,
Thy track is mark'd by one long line of death.
By thee the emerald sea is stain'd with blood,
That spreads its crimson cloud along the flood:
Fierce as the loudest thunder bursts thy roar—
Thy worst of lightnings cleave the fated shore!
From thee earth's best and bravest meet their doom;
And nations form one universal tomb:

The mangled lie upon the ground to groan—
The dying writhe, and pour th' unheeded moan ;
While distant friendship breathes the fruitless prayer
For him who bleeds to death, unaided there.
Man, and his hopes, together pass from day ;
While anguish rends the thread of life away :
Or driv'n a wand'rer from his earliest home,
But lives an outcast o'er the world to roam.

What desolation is around thee seen !
What hopeless wreck where'er thy rout hath been !
A needful evil, if indeed thou art,
They who provoke thee, least endure thy smart!
The tears of orphans in thy footsteps flow ;
Thy tread but echoes to the widow's woe ;
Science before thy swift destruction flies ;
And art in ruin sinks, and commerce dies :
The muses fly to some calm, peaceful shore ;
And agriculture tills the ground no more :
The worst of passions in thy train appear ;
And ghastly famine closes up the rear.

Forcing man back to barbarous days again,
His path of light is darken'd by thy reign :
The works of genius, and of time, expire ;
Life's charms are lost, and joy and hope retire.

Thus when Vesuvius pours her fires around,
And sudden desolation whelms the ground;
Flames sweep away the valley's lovely bloom,
And sink the fruits of labor to the tomb. .

Urburgh! thou seat of glory, and of bliss—
Could nothing save thee from a doom like this!
Alas! and could not riches—valor—all
That renders nations safe, prevent thy fall!
What—when thy sword, that scarce was drawn in vain,
Was winning empire on some distant plain—
When over far-off seas thy thunders flash'd;
And hostile fleets beneath their surges dash'd—
While half the world still named thee with alarm—
Was fate to wither thy undaunted arm;
And strike thee down, 'ere time had stol'n thy power;
And shed this darkness on thy noontide hour!
So have I seen, in manhood's strength and bloom,
Death's victim hurried to a sudden tomb.
But why in anguish should I linger here,
Where every object but provokes a tear?
O'erwhelming sorrow bids me shun the view,
Thou early lov'd— my native spot—adieu!
But still, whatever realm salutes mine eyes,

Thy cherish'd beauties will in memory rise ;

The brightest scenes that earth to me can show,

Compared with thee, will prove a waste of woe ;

Along whatever clime my feet may rove,

Thou still wilt live the idol of my love :

Long as I breathe—however far I stray—

My heart is here, nor will be torn away ;

To thee my fondness must be ever true ;

My home—my hope—my native scene, adieu !

END OF THE DESERTED CITY.

EVA.

CANTO THE FIRST.

EVA.

CANTO I.

I.

Poets have sung of beauty, till the theme,
But for its infinite variety,
Would pall the hearer like an oft-told dream:
No charms have shone—of colour—symmetry—
That have so often been man's bliss to see ;
Which pen and pencil have not tried to trace—
The eye in all its silent witchery !
The mighty magic of the perfect face—
And forms that lightly moved with every living grace.

II.

Yet hath there o'er the mental vision past,

The more than earthly charms of shape and eye ;

And have such fascination round them cast,

In life—to see—and lose them—were to die!

In vain the Poet's highest efforts try

To give to others' ken those forms reveal'd,

That burst on him in lightning, but defy

The pencilling of language—that must yield,

And leave perfection still to blaze in fancy's field.

III.

And such was Eva! form than hers more fair,

Ne'er floated in the golden flood of light :

Lips sweeter—lovelier—never breath'd the air ;

Nor eyes so softly blue, and yet so bright,

Shed such intoxication on the sight :

Like diamonds in a limpid brook they seem'd,

Darting their colours through its veil of white;

And shining but the clearer as it stream'd :

So set in liquid light, her orbs of azure beam'd.

IV.

Yet it was not her lovely eye, that shone
Full, bright, and blue as heaven's unclouded sky—
'Twas not her angel countenance alone,
Nor any single charm that caught the eye,
Won where it thought to pass unsmitten by—
It was that harmonizing, perfect whole,
Which might with beauties cull'd from thousands vie;
That shed such full delight upon the soul,
And captive held the heart, spite of the will's controul.

V.

And she was innocence itself! her heart
Ne'er harbour'd one impure, unholy thought;
Her breast ne'er knew a wish—which to impart
Might force a blush across her cheek, nor aught
Beyond what vestal virtue might have taught:
Attuned to finest feeling, every nerve
With chastest sensibility was fraught;
Which in her warmest moments, did but serve
To guide her in the path from which she might not swerve.

VI.

Cold to herself, not others ; she had been
    Full oft' observ'd to shed the genuine tear,
    When she had sought some sad and gloomy scene,
    To sooth the pangs of sorrow or of fear :
    She, with unenvying pleasure, thrill'd to hear
    Of aught that made another's happiness :
    The joy of others seem'd to her as dear
    As that she found her own pure soul to bless,
The seat of feeling, truth, and angel loveliness.

VII.

It was her pleasure up the steep to climb,
    When the gray morn led on the golden day
    Over the eastern hills ; to view sublime
    The opening landscape, that around her lay,
    While the dim mists, slow melting, roll'd away :
    To see the silver lake, the ceaseless stream,
    Awaking in the dancing light to play ;
    While trembling dew-drops caught the glittering beam,
And seem'd upon the eye in fields of gems to gleam.

VIII.

She sat in silent adoration there,

Till the unwearied sun was thron'd on high ;

Breathing the fragrant and untainted air,

And feasting on the scene that fill'd her eye ;

Where earth seem'd turn'd to gold beneath the sky ;

Where every tint creation wears, appear'd

To robe the world, and her rich canopy :

Till lovely nature grew the more endear'd,

And through her beauteous works her Author more
rever'd.

IX.

Where the thick wood hung darkly over head,

Till scarce a ray reliev'd the shadow'd ground;

Where tangled shrubs their mingled foliage spread,

And noontide twilight seem'd to reign around ;

Lone in its deepest shades she might be found,

Tracing the charms of nature's hidden store,

That else had lived and died in that profound,

Ungather'd and unseen, but lov'd the more

For the retiring forms, and modest hues they wore.

X.

None was more fond than she, when noon was shot,
To cull the fairest of the garden's pride;
The blushing beauties of each favor'd spot,
  With every deep and soften'd colour dyed;
These, in a lovely, fragrant cluster tied,
She placed to decorate the lonely room
Where mourn'd her Father for his buried bride;
Who, smitten in perfection—pluck'd in bloom—
Was wrested from his arms, an offering to the tomb.

XI.

Eva had many a deep and burning thought,
Within her glowing, half-enthusiast mind:
With that wild, energetic fervour, fraught,
That few would think in form so fair to find!
They were not light, nor fleeting, but divined
The mysteries that common souls glide o'er;
Profoundest truths, of deep and awful kind—
The wonders of created things—the lore
Of nature, 'midst her vast and inexhaustless store.

XII.

Though few can see with apathy of eye,

Th' expanse of stars that roof the arch of night ;

None e'er contemplated the scene on high,

With vaster thoughts arising from the sight!

She saw not merely glittering gems of light—

But worlds, that in illimitable space

Roll'd their unerring round in ceaseless flight ;

And suns, whose planets ne'er reveal'd their place,

Whose beings and whose scenes, her fancy burn'd to

trace.

XIII.

And most she loved to stray, when Dian's beam

Pour'd down in soften'd light—in some deep glen

To sit, and see her silver arrows stream

Betwixt the whispering foliage, that then

Waved o'er her, happy that no vulgar ken

Beheld her transports, that no mortal ear

O'erheard her self-communion, which dull men

Had folly deem'd ; and blest to think the tear

She shed in rapture, fell, and dried where none were near.

XIV.

And often in that solitude were heard
Melodious sounds, that through night's shadows
      rung—
(The wond'ring listener stopp'd—nor breath'd, nor
      stirr'd—
But stood all ear, as if some seraph sung;
And round his sweetly trembling echoes flung—)
Rising from out that depth in harmony,
As fabled Sirens erst, with magic tongue,
Pour'd their bewitching music o'er the sea—
Hers shed as much delight, but left no misery.

XV.

But there was sorrow when its dying tone
Expired, as if some joyous dream were o'er;
The listener felt abandon'd and alone,
Like one left lonely on a desert shore;
But still he linger'd, hoping it might pour
Again its soul inspiring music round;
Praying to hear that heavenly strain once more;
Trembling in sweetness, till the full, rich sound,
Th' intoxicated sense in spell of magic bound.

XVI.

Nought is so sweet as music heard at night,

After the tumult of the toiling day ;

When the eye scarcely feels the loss of light,

Nor marks the western twilight's setting ray :

It seems to draw the barb of grief away ;

Leaving the thrill of happiness behind ;

And proves one sense alone, in joyous play,

Hath power to tranquillize and bless the mind,

Rapt, as if all the rest were in that one combin'd.

XVII.

Near where her Father's rural mansion stood,

(Screen'd by a hill and half embower'd in trees—)

Hung o'er a glassy lake's expanding flood,

A Castle's ruins caught the murmuring breeze :

In its drear chambers fancied fears might seize

The starting form that traced their shadowy gloom.

Few found in its dark grandeur aught to please ;

But in its caverns saw the living tomb,

Where met the prison'd wretch his swift or lingering doom.

XVIII.

In lonely desolation frowning high,

Above the vale so vast a shade it spread,

It might be deem'd a cloud hung o'er the sky,

To intercept the light that morning shed :

More awful in its solitude, its head

Was veil'd in clouds that damp'd it as they past :

'Twas view'd by passing peasants with that dread

The fearful tales of bygone centuries cast ;

Till groans in fancy's ear seem'd mingling with the blast.

XIX.

Though it was founded on the granite rock—

Not ev'n that rock itself resists decay—

Though age had turn'd its walls to flint ; the shock

Of elements was wasting them away !

Time stole unseen its fragments day by day ;

Exposed to all the warring winds of heaven,

And beating rain ; of fiercest storms the prey,

That full against its battlements were driven ;

Their ceaseless efforts wore what thunder scarce had
    riven.

XX.

Though half in wreck, enough was left to tell
What in its day of pride that pile had been;
In ruin terrible, it spoke too well
Of many a wild, and dark, and cruel scene;
When murder stalk'd its prison walls between:
Its deep and massy dungeons seem'd to speak
The deeds of slaughter—they were formed to screen;
Whose arches rung with many a desperate shriek;
When dying victims bore all tyrant hate could wreak.

XXI.

Yes! they might shriek—but through those flinty walls
Of sorrow or of madness past no sound;
The writhing sufferer's agonizing calls
Burst unavailing in that dread profound;
Their life's last drop might stiffen on that ground,
Yet redden not on man's attesting eye;
Their bones might whiten where they fell around,
Nor flash one proof of crime but to the sky—
Unseen—untomb'd—unpitied—unarranged to lie!

XXII.

Such hath it ever been since life began,
That man of his own race hath been the foe;
With ruffian violence, or wily plan,
To wring, to trample, and to lay him low;
To force his groans to burst, his tears to flow—
And but that some have liv'd who would not swell,
But mitigate, the other's work of woe—
This world, where such remorseless beings dwell,
Had been a den of guilt, and less like earth than hell.

XXIII.

Eva's was all the spirit of romance;
She often toil'd that Castle's steep ascent;
And traced, in fancy, glittering sword and lance
Gleam through its courts, as once, when loud shouts
    rent
Its echoing walls, with clashing weapons blent:
The tramp of war, the clattering of arms;
The wrath of its besiegers, idly spent;
The marshalling of bands; the loud alarms;
Successive past her mind, in fancy's magic charms:

XXIV.

The gorgeous pastime and high festival;
The banquet scene of desperate revelry,
That shook the armour-decorated hall;
The friendly fierceness of proud chivalry;
The roar of half intoxicated glee,
When lord and vassal mingled at the board—
While minstrels woke the chords of harmony;
When all that joy could ask, or power afford,
Was spread—nor scarce was spar'd the war-devoted
    hoard.

XXV.

But now there was no sound of living thing;
Save when the night-bird, startled from her sleep,
Toil'd through the gloom with heavy flapping wing,
Breaking with moans the silence dread and deep,
That seem'd its breathless empire there to keep:
Nor voice, nor tread, proclaim'd that life was there;
The eye that loved the haunts of man, might weep
To see the desolation and despair,
That reign'd betwixt those walls; damp, tenantless,
    and bare.

XXVI.

There she embodied those dark histories
In childhood often heard with wond'ring ear,
As present seen—living realities—
Saw them as passing—but devoid of fear:
Treading its galleries, long, dark, and drear;
She seem'd to share the deeds of days gone by;
She gave each fancied sufferer the tear;
For long departed captives breath'd the sigh;
As rapt in musings deep, each figure fill'd her eye.

XXVII.

Each passage—chamber—dungeon—as she past,
Her tread in hollow echoes flung around ;
But in the midnight shadows that they cast,
No form to wake one throb of dread she found ;
She fear'd no spectre, gliding without sound—
'Twas the romantic feeling that arose
From that wild scene, to make the pulses bound,
The spirit thrill—it was for this she chose
In fancy to revive its grandeur and its woes.

XXVIII.

She did not shudder when in hollow moans
The wind rush'd howling through those avenues;
Rising and sinking, like expiring groans,
That well in weaker minds might fear infuse;
Yet did but o'er her ardent mind diffuse
A wild and awful thrill—intense delight
Rose from its loneliness and solemn hues!
Perchance it raised her fancy to a height
Unsafe to wing, because it veil'd life's truths from sight.

XXIX.

But none can tell, who know not such high feeling,
The secret joys of such wild solitude;
What undefinable sensations stealing,
Entrance the mind in that romantic mood:
When thoughts are cherish'd, and when scenes are
      view'd,
That own no tie to earth, nor life can show;
When every grov'ling passion sinks subdued;
When the soul seems to snap its chain below,
Rapt in the extacies that none but such can know.

XXX.

There was at home one sacred—little spot,
Eva most idolized, and oftenest sought :
No day unvisited—no hour forgot—
Where in the garden's deepest shade was wrought
A Mother's monument; to which she brought
The fairest of that garden's flowers, to strew
Around the urn.　With pious sorrow fraught;
The tears she shed refresh'd them like the dew,
While many a bitter thought across her bosom flew.

XXXI.

Those thoughts she loved to cherish, though they sent
A feeling of bereavement through her soul :
She lov'd to rouse that sorrow, though it rent;
And once awaken'd, spurn'd the will's controul :
Though but to see that spot was woe—she stole
To ponder there, as 'twere a place of rest;
Whose sight, instead of wounding, might console !
Lean'd on it as it were a mother's breast—
View'd it as though her eye that mother's form possess'd.

XXXII.

It was possess'd—as if that stone had breath,
She there felt not alone: that cherish'd form
Floated around the urn that spoke her death,
As if the very marble seem'd to warm
Beneath her gaze—as though she could transform
To breathing life that sculptur'd shape of woe!
As if recover'd from the feasting worm,
The buried started forth again to glow;
Past tenderness, and faith, and loveliness, to show.

XXXIII.

And every tree of dark and mournful hue
Hung over it—the cypress cast its shade;
Above it waved the melancholy yew,
As if its foliage there a pall had made;
The drooping willow by its side display'd
Its pendant branches, as in sorrow hung;
Behind its lonely seat, a dark stream stray'd
The deeply rooted trees and shrubs among:
Amidst whose leaves the wind its plaintive murmurs flung.

XXXIV.

'Twas evening—all around was soft, serene;
No breath among the branches seem'd to play;
Not ev'n a leaf was moving in the scene;
The Sun was sinking gorgeously away,
And crimson curtains veil'd the close of day:
The golden clouds that slumber'd in the sky,
Stretch'd out like ocean's waves in bright array;
Edg'd with the lingering rays that glanc'd from high,
Over the western hills, to gild them to the eye.

XXXV.

The lake was still; not ev'n a dimple past
Across its surface, where reflected seem'd
Another world to lie, as two were cast
From out one mould, so perfectly it gleam'd:
There the trees spread their branches, and there
    stream'd
The many-colour'd clouds, as bright—as fair;
Another setting sun as redly beam'd;
Cot shone, and mountain threw its shadow there,
As motionless as those that rais'd their tops in air.

XXXVI.

'Twas evening—she was leaning on that tomb,
Pond'ring a mother's look—a mother's love!
An eye was turn'd upon her through the gloom,
Whose glance might well the strongest feelings move—
She started—strain'd her eye towards th' alcove
That hid the mystic form that look who sent—
'Twas gone—there past a sigh—in vain she strove
To see its utterer—deep'ning twilight lent
No ray to mark his form, nor trace the path he went.

XXXVII.

What did he there? approach'd he as a spy
Upon her lonely, meditating hour?
Or was it rather with arrested eye
He fascinated hung on beauty's power;
And sought unfear'd, unwitness'd, to devour
The charms which bloom'd in that sequester'd place;
To gaze in secret on that guarded flower;
The beauty of its tint and form to trace;
And worship, (though unseen,) its pure and matchless
grace.

XXXVIII.

She left that spot—nor was it all in fear;
She turn'd—and turn'd again, with searching eye—
Her father greeted—but her absent ear
Heard but the fancied echo of that sigh;
That glance of fascination still was nigh;
'Twas in her dreams in all its mystery;
She scarce would chase it—and it did not fly—
Who might that gazer—what his purpose be?
Who, spite of better thoughts, had work'd this witchery.

XXXIX.

'Twas the first time that ever living form
Had rais'd within her bosom such emotion;
'Twas the first time that eye could e'er so warm
Her heart, or rouse her thoughts to such commotion;
Now restless as the waves of troubled ocean—
'Twas the first time she ever felt within
The spirit's earthly object of devotion—
And if such worship be a fault—a sin—
O who may ever hope a future heaven to win!

XL.

That eye had such inscrutable expression
As language could define not—but 'twas felt
At heart beyond the power of repression ;
Where it but once had lighted, there it dwelt,
Until the coldest feelings seem'd to melt
Beneath its penetrating influence ;
Till soften'd and subdued the victim knelt,
Resigning every thought, and every sense,
To that new tyrant power it could not banish thence.

XLI.

Though it might be that dim and dubious light
In which she saw it, clothed it with a power
It had not own'd if blazing on the sight
In noon's transcendant, all-displaying hour—
But no—the night might darken—morning lour—
Its light was in itself, nor e'er could fail :
'Twould flash amidst the tempest and the shower ;
No time could dim it, and no shadows veil,
From one whose spell-bound soul it purpos'd to assail.

XLII.

Morn found her on that spot again—but why
She scarcely knew—it was not that she sought
That stranger form—she was too pure and high,
To cherish so unfeminine a thought—
But there she was; and now that place seem'd fraught
With an increased, unusual interest;
As if her soul new inspiration caught
From thence, which glowing, thrilling in her breast,
Prov'd something still might be to doom her curst or
     blest.

XLIII.

He was not there—but on the ground there lay
A picture—dropt by chance, or left to tell
Who had been there—and that she might survey
Its features, till they work'd into a spell—
She grasp'd it breathlessly—she knew full well
Th' expressive eye she view'd but to adore !
Though seen but once, yet ever more to dwell
In fancy and remembrance, till it wore
All feelings, thoughts, away, that cherish'd were before.

XLIV.

She gazed—till line and lineament devour'd,
Sunk like a honey'd poison in her soul—
Till reason fail'd, bewilder'd and o'erpower'd;
And treacherous intoxication stole
Through every sense, defying all controul.
She ponder'd on that eye's bewitching beam;
That manly check; that fascinating whole—
Till her half-conscious reveries might seem
The wonder-working sport of some romantic dream.

XLV.

How long she gazed—herself alone might know;
How oft she started, lest some eye the while
Might fancy in her features love's warm glow,
None else could say—It was not that her smile—
Her blush—she deem'd were aught that could defile
Her soul, or stain its virgin purity;
But pride might slander—prudery revile—
Her bosom told her there was extacy;
Which, since none else could judge—she would none
      else should see.

XLVI.

But such is woman! mystery at best!
Seeming most cold when most her heart is burning—
Hiding the melting passions of her breast
Beneath a snowy cloud, and scarce returning
One glance on him, for whom her soul is yearning :
Adoring, yet repelling—proud, but weak—
Conquer'd—commanding still; enslav'd—yet spurn-
    ing :
Checking the words her heart would bid her speak ;
Love raging in her breast, but banish'd from her cheek.

XLVII.

He who would read her thoughts, must mark unseen
Her eyes' full, undisguised expression ; trace—
(If trace he could, while distance stretch'd between)—
The feelings blushing, quivering, on her face :
He who would know her heart, must first embrace,
And feel it beat uncheck'd against his own ;
Chill'd not by pride, nor fear ; nor time, nor place—
As in a dream·—unwitness'd and alone;
When every fearful thought unconsciously has flown.

XLVIII.

That picture, now the partner of her walk,
She gazed on, till its features seem'd to move—
Until its pencill'd lips appear'd to talk,
And its eyes beam the speaking looks of love;
Whether in sunshine, or the twilight grove—
Not now, as once, alone she seem'd to stray;
However far her wand'ring feet might rove,
He still was there, the sharer of her day;
As though a living form beneath that image lay.

XLIX,

But what is all the pencil's power to trace,
With all the lustre colour can bestow,
The workings of the soul that light the face—;
The changing passions—these it cannot show—
Nor aught but the same form of joy or woe;
The shape, the hue of feature, may be there—
It is but death vermilion'd ! cheeks may glow,
But ne'er turn pale ; there lacks the speaking air—
The transient smile and tear—th' alternate hope—
despair.

L.

Sad through the ruins sigh'd the evening wind ;
Eva sat listening to its plaintive moan :
A pleasing melancholy thrill'd her mind :
She deem'd—but scarcely felt herself alone—
Sudden there stole upon her ear the tone
Of distant harmony ! That place before
To her ne'er echo'd utterance but her own :
In all her visits she ne'er found it bore
One other soul, the strain of joy or grief to pour.

LI.

She started, wondering whose that voice might be,
That broke the silence with so sweet a sound—
Whether it were some spirit's minstrelsy;
Or warblings of a soul that sought and found
Peace—safety—in the solitude around :
Some spirit that the world had wrung to madness—
Some heart, that man had trampled to the ground ;
That sought unheard, unseen, to vent its sadness ;
Hoping in secrecy to find some gleam of gladness.

LII.

Now dying distant, and now swelling near;
Its sound among the hollow arches hung—
Before one note expir'd upon the ear,
Another, following its echoes, flung
Its mingling strain, as though two voices sung:
: Now full and strong, its utterer might be deem'd
Some bard inspired—and now so sweet it rung—
Softer than woman's softest tone it seem'd,
As with the very soul of harmony it teem'd.

LIII.

It drew her near it with unconscious tread—
She knew no evil, and she fear'd no ill;
Yet trod as if a sound might wake the dead;
Intent upon those melting strains, that still
Seem'd not th' ear only, but the soul to fill;
Till near enough to see, her eye beheld
A form that caused her panting heart to thrill—
She gazed till extacy her bosom swell'd;
And rising passion, spite of sense and will, rebell'd.

LIV.

She saw a form of more than manly grace;
Perfect in symmetry of shape and limb;
Winning—but nothing feminine, that face
On which she look'd till sight grew almost dim,
And her bewilder'd senses seem'd to swim—
That form—that air—she could not doubt 'twas he!
She saw—she felt—at last she gazed on him,
Whose image she had ponder'd secretly;
When she scarce thought or wish'd his living self to see.

LV.

The light stream'd on him from a space above;
The glow of evening on his features fell;
His eye—his countenance—were form'd for love:
The scene—the hour—conspired to work the spell,
That drew its circle round her heart too well.
She caught the words that warbled in his song;
Whose tone and accent seem'd at once to tell
Some inly-cherish'd passion, deep and strong,
Which bore thought, feeling, all—tumultuously along.

As a rose in the desert that blooms almost lost,
  As a jewel that fate had been kind to conceal;
I have look'd on the lovely one—gazed to my cost;
  But cannot, and dare not, affection reveal;
Though my soul in a whirlwind of passion is tost,
  She knows not the pangs she has caused me to feel.

As nothing that nature hath form'd can compare
  With the bloom of her cheek, and the light of her eye—
As another ne'er flourish'd so perfectly fair;
  Nor can scarcely be hoped as a boon from the sky—
So no tempest can equal my depth of despair;
  Though it blacken below, and roll thunder on high.

Though I saw her but once -'twas enough to impart,
  In the hope of her love, the intenseness of joy;
A moment were even too much for the heart,
  To endure the despair that must quickly destroy—
Yet that one deep impression can never depart,
  But my soul must in bliss or in anguish employ.

LVI.

Though ceas'd the strain; yet still did Eva seem
Its past bewitching harmony to feel;
Like the sweet memory of some pleasing dream.
He cross'd her path—as lightning turns to steel
Their glances met; but what they might reveal—
Who could unfold—since man doth oft' assume
Passions he feels not—woman her's conceal;
So much, that lovers scarcely know their doom;
Whether the bridal wreath, or passion's early tomb.

LVII.

They met—but past not unregarding by—
They met—but not like strangers, though unknown—
Their introduction was the speaking eye—
A welcome greeted in the look alone;
Where mute surprize and pleasure mingled shone—
Needless are words when souls congenial meet;
If no disguise be o'er the features thrown,
The face with eloquence is so replete,
That speech could little more than what it told repeat.

LVIII.

At times 'twould seem as if the judgment sate

In wisdom thron'd within the searching eye ;

Whose intuition dooms if love or hate

Should be the meed of him who passeth by :

As inspiration lent its power to try

His heart—as if it lay exposed and bare ;

While every thought, wish, feeling—seem to lie

Unveil'd before those piercing glances there ;

Which he so judg'd might deem were hid with closest
care.

LIX.

And O ! though falsehood may at times deceive—

Oft' is that instantaneous sentence right !

Though passion, wilful—blind—will scarce believe

The fiat that the soul proclaims at sight,

But turns from day, and is betray'd by night ;

Till time dissolves the mist, and truth relumes

Her radiant torch, and reigns enthron'd in light ;

Pierces the mask hypocrisy assumes,

And hideous, naked vice, to scorn and loathing dooms.

LX.

One look alone had beam'd—and they were friends—
Half lovers at the second—from their eyes
Flash'd the pure, bright intelligence, that tends
To show, or win a soul—the sympathies
That light the face, uncurtain'd by disguise;
When the heart's secret, on the changing cheek,
To him who bears a brow as open, lies—
The quivering lip, though silent, still may speak;
When words are wanted not—or if they came, were weak.

LXI.

He walk'd beside her to her father's door;
There breath'd, as from his soul, a soft good-night.
The ground had ne'er seem'd passed so soon before—
She never felt so much the loss of light,
For now the darkness veil'd him from her sight,
Though his slow sounding steps still reach'd her ear.
She had not check'd him like a prude—nor quite
Indulged him with a smile; but free from fear,
In conscious innocence, reck'd not what eyes were near.

LXII.

The child of nature, what she felt she show'd,
As far as female purity may do;
Her glances froze not when her bosom glow'd—
When joy was in her heart, her features too
Smiled; and her eyes display'd a brighter blue;
What she might blush to look, she fear'd to feel:
Nothing like those, who, thoughts of darkest hue
Forbid the struggling visage to reveal—
But in a living mask their infamy conceal:

LXIII.

Yet these at times forget disguise—the heart
Will force despite its blackness on the face;
Nor, does th' unwelcome cloud at will depart;
Some demon passion will too often trace
Its furious passage o'er that treacherous place,
And flash unbidden lightnings from the eye!
In spite of guile, thoughts—feelings—fierce and base,
To the betraying countenance will fly;
As sudden storms arise, and sweep the placid sky.

G

LXIV.

And Leon, (such the name he bore,) was one
Might soon attune to love a woman's soul;
He vanquish'd ere his purpose seem'd begun;
So silently into the mind he stole—
Fixing his empire there above controul;
So imperceptibly he won his way
Into the heart, whose conquest was his goal;
Which, e'er it fear'd his power, confess'd his sway;
And found him rooted there, to bless or to betray.

LXV.

The next day saw him at her father's board,
To whom his name, his lineage, once was known:
Next evening by her side with joy he pour'd
The rapture in his kindling face that shone—
He seem'd awake to love, and love alone;
The magnet of his eye was Eva's face;
His ear seem'd closed to all but Eva's tone; ·
As with insatiate sight he gazed to trace
Uncloying loveliness, and still increasing grace.

LXVI.

Romantic bosoms soonest feel the power
Of love, and feel it at its fiercest height;
While weaker spirits plod their dull, cold hour:
The highest trees are soonest topp'd with light—
Are first to meet the tempest in its flight—
And fall, wrench'd, crush'd, and levell'd by the blast—
While the low shrub, that scarcely meets the sight,
Survives, to flourish when the storm is past;
Above whose bending head its wrath was idly cast.

LXVII.

The widest ocean rolls the vastest waves—
The deepest sea is last to sink to rest—
So when in man the storm of passion raves,
Its wildest throb is in the mightiest breast;
There soonest blazes, and is last represt!
The depth of feeling, and the range of thought—
Th' omnipotence of spirit—is imprest
On all it shows; whether with rapture fraught,
Or in its bursting rage to maniac fury wrought.

LXVIII.

But 'tis not every face, nor eye, can move,
(However fair—however bright they be—)
Beings of that superior stamp to love !
Such seek a spirit of like energy ;
From plodding thoughts, and earthborn feelings free !
No face they worship where they do not find—
No eye admire in which they do not see—
The path of thought, the lightning of the mind ;
Whose vivid impress leaves form, colour, far behind.

LXIX.

When beings of that favor'd order meet,
Both flourishing in youth and loveliness ;
When, not the tongue, but souls that kindle, greet—
Looking what language never could express—
'Tis then that love must madden or must bless !
'Tis there that passion lights its fiercest fire—
Burns equal to the spirit's mightiness !
While every feeling, sense, and thought, conspire
To feed that master flame—that one intense desire.

LXX.

Such souls were their's—though both forbore to speak,
　Each saw in each the simultaneous thought;
Eye answer'd eye, and cheek replied to cheek,
　As both at once the same idea caught;
As their two forms were with one spirit fraught—
　Whether they turn'd on earth the wond'ring eye,
Or, to enthusiastic fervor wrought,
　When Dian lit her silver lamp on high,
Peopled the glittering orbs that gemm'd the trackless sky.

LXXI.

His mind was strength and brilliance—her's the sweet,
　The soften'd lustre of a milder light;
He, like the noontide sun, whose blaze and heat
　Spreads fiercely when no cloud obscures the sight;
Shone out in all the force of mental might—
　She beam'd the beauties of his evening ray,
When clouds of gold and crimson herald night—
　His was the fulness of the perfect day—
Her's was its beauteous blush, before it sinks away.

LXXII.

To every eye the moonlight scene is sweet,
But most of all to lovers when they stray;
Yielding just light enough to guide their feet,
But not for prying eyes to watch their way—
Sufficient to unfold the smiles that play,
Through its transparent gauze, on beauty's face;
Showing the features soften'd by its ray:
It not denies the eye their charms to trace,
But o'er their lustre sheds a milder, softer grace.

LXXII..

The triumph then is that of form alone,
When bank—tree—hill—display their outline fair;
When colours, lost, or blended all in one,
Scarce leave the eye a wish to find them there—
All things are figur'd in the pale blue air;
Though nothing can a dazzling brightness show;
The dancing waters shine, but do not glare;
The cheek is lovely, though it does not glow,
And eyes that flash at noon, there silver glances throw.

LXXIV.

Pure is the joy at such an hour to rove;
Whether it be to breathe in Beauty's ear
The murmuring whispers of accepted love;
Or with a friend, firm, ardent, and sincere;
When souls congenial know each other dear—
The mind oft' wakes at the approach of night:
As if it strove its lustre should appear,
(When earthly objects darken on the sight,)
To pierce its deep'ning shades with inly-kindled light.

LXXV.

And Eva's days past swiftly as a dream,
When health has tuned the pulse to joyous play;
The rapid flight of time did scarcely seem
To wait the dawn—the noon—the close of day—
But sped, as in a meteor flash, away—
As bright—as transient—as the bliss it brought!
Hours swiftest fly from those who wish their stay;
And linger longest where their boon is nought
But grief, despair, and pain; and ever-wearing thought.

LXXVI.

Who never loved, hath lost earth's highest bliss—
Who never felt its thrill—its sting—can know
Nothing of that where life's chief pleasure is !
The brightest days that man enjoys below,
Are those that pass in its inspiring glow ;
When new sensations seem to wake the soul
As to a second being—to bestow
Thoughts, feelings, hopes, that bound beyond controul ;
And show in this dark world, at least one joyous goal.

LXXVII.

What though it may at times the bosom wring—
There is a rapture even in its pain !
What though it leave a deep, and burning sting—
The wounded heart will wake to joy again ;
As hope—despair—alternate rule maintain :
A bitter pleasure mingles with the sigh,
The breather would not, if he could, restrain—
And ev'n the tear that rushes to the eye,
Comes a half-welcome guest, that soothes while trick-
    ling by.

LXXVIII.

Where is the lover would his pangs forego?
What doating heart craves unimpassion'd peace?
Who loves the cause of sorrow—clasps the woe—
Nor scarce would wish the frequent sigh should cease;
Nor from such willing thraldom ask release:
When he, perchance, might draw th' envenom'd dart,
He leaves it rankling, though his pangs increase;
Until the fest'ring wound, and burning smart,
Corrode the springs of life, and waste away the heart.

LXXIX.

And what is reason, when oppos'd to love?
What though the object might be justly spurn'd,
As shorn of truth or virtue—nought can move
The heart that doats; crimes—follies—not discern'd,
Or heeded not—affection not return'd—
Nothing can shake its madness from the mind!
For this ambition, that for empire burn'd,
Hath lost a throne; to shame—destruction—blind!
Friends—country—home—all good, it leaves despised
behind.

LXXX.

Eva had named the day to make them one—
If more united they could ever be,
Whose souls to mingle had at first begun ;
Whose feelings seem'd to move in unity :
She show'd in her silent looks; and he
Breath'd it in all the eloquence of speech—
Time roll'd to stamp unceasing constancy ;
  Each seem'd to live to prove the joy of each ;
Secure as if no shaft of ill their hearts could reach.

END OF THE FIRST CANTO.

EVA.

CANTO THE SECOND.

EVA.

I.

ALAS! how bounded is the sight of man!
Though dreaming he can pierce futurity—
The very morrow blasts his cherish'd plan:
This hour in hope—the next in misery!
A sudden tempest brings his destiny—
Secure, while ruin lies but just before him:
The bolt of death he hears not—nor can see:
Self-flatter'd ev'n while darkness gathers o'er him;
Till sunk within th' abyss, whence nothing can restore
   him.

II.

Eva one morn was missing from her home ;
And Leon travers'd each accustom'd spot ;
Trod every track he knew she lov'd to roam—
The wood—the ruins—each contiguous cot—
The borders of the lake—but found her not :
Explor'd the mountain to its snowy peak—
No path she used to wander was forgot ;
She was not there—and o'er his blanching cheek
There past a chilling fear he would not—dared not
       speak.

III.

Past from her father's board th' untasted meal—
He sought his child in anguish deep and wild !
Parents alone can judge what he must feel ;
Nor they—save they have lost an only child !
He cried—" Some fell destroyer hath beguil'd—
But no ! impossible ! her heart so pure,
So firm, would never live to be defil'd—
Would rather death in all its worst endure !—
She may be tortur'd—slain—her innocence is sure."

IV.

Leon return'd at noon—but came alone—
'Twas but one word—one deep emphatic—" No!"
His tongue could utter—but its withering tone
Had in it all the eloquence of woe!
All he said not his anguish'd looks might show.
Both stood the living statues of depair!
The father spake not—not a tear would flow—
That proof of weaker sorrow came not there,
It was a burning woe, that no relief could share.

V.

And Leon scarce could bear to see the place,
Where his heart-cherish'd idol should have been;
Who gave it every joy, and every grace;
The very hope and spirit of the scene—
'Twas like earth blasted—reft of all her green!
Cold—dreary—lifeless—sunless—desolate !
Where if one beam of day the eye could glean,
It serv'd but to depict the bliss that Fate
Once blest the heart with there, before she launch'd her
hate.

VI.

He wander'd long and lonely—evening came—
But Eva came not—nothing could controul
His anguish—though the day went down in flame,
'Twas darkness—midnight darkness to his soul!
The stars came brightly out—he saw them roll—
They only show'd she gazed not with him there!
And for her absence nothing could console!
Nothing was joyous that she did not share—
He felt alone on earth—abandon'd to despair!

VII.

The night grew deeper—darkness stole along—
Nor sight nor sound of Eva could he gain :
Grief, fear, and disappointment, grew so strong,
They raged almost to madness through his brain!
He strain'd his eyes to pierce the shades in vain—
In vain her name burst from his fever'd tongue;
His anxious ear could no return obtain ;
Though loud from hill to hill the accents rung,
No answering sound arose their solitudes among.

VIII.

That night, nor sire nor lover pillow prest—
It was a night of horror—not repose;
An agony of thought, cut off from rest:
The eye might in its socket burn, but close
It could not—overwhelm'd in woes,
The father paced his echoing room; the lover
Sought every spot where fancy might suppose
A hope remain'd his Eva to discover;
Urging the useless search, till night and hope were over.

IX.

Sleep! sleep may be for those whose hearts, though aching,
            aching,
Have still some hope, that, spite of all, they keep—
But not for those that in despair are breaking :
Those eyes may be revisited by sleep,
That still have tears—refreshing tears to weep—
Not those that have none left, but burn to madness !
Slumber comes not to pangs so wild and deep;
Though it may settle on the brow of sadness,
And ev'n forerun a day of calm and gentle gladness.

X.

Sleep! no—insensibility alone
Could find it in that scene of woe and dread;
The breast that then could slumber, must be stone!
Sleep might as soon its placid influence shed
On him, who feels an earthquake lift his bed;
Or sees the charg'd volcano scorch the sky,
And burning rivers round his dwelling spread;
Or heav'd upon the angry waves on high,
With scarce a moment left to know that he must die.

XI.

And yet the robber sleeps upon his spoil!
The murd'rer on his bloody hand can rest—
Nor terror nor remorse their slumbers foil;
As if the couch of innocence they prest,
Or conscience were no inmate of the breast;
While he whose guiltless heart is rent by grief,
Can scarce in its forgetfulness be blest;
To whom it oft denies that short relief
It ev'n vouchsafes to give the slayer and the thief!

XII.

Oh! how unlike the bosoms of mankind!
Some on no living thing bestow a tear;
Their feelings all within themselves enshrin'd—
Some weep if but a wounded bird appear—
Some quaff the goblet on a father's bier!
Where other eyes would weep their orbs away,
Some gaze in apathy, as nought were near—
Some live to feel for others, day by day;
Some are but breathing stones, that feeling ne'er betray.

XIII.

Succeeding years of bliss could scarce atone
The Father's horrors through that long, drear night:
He thought it never—never would be done—
And yet he scarce had hope that with the light
His child would come again, to bless his sight!
He told the clock—how long before its sound
Would strike his ear again! in wild affright
He listen'd from his casement—but profound
Silence prevail'd, save when the night-wind mourn'd
    around.

XIV.

Far better to behold the bed of death;
And the last moments of a loved one see—
To gaze upon the form, though reft of breath,
Than weep its loss in dubious misery;
Upon the rack to know its destiny—
Whether still left on earth, or in the grave—
Tortur'd to frenzy by uncertainty;
Ign'rant what path might lead to find, or save;
Though willing in that search the worst of ills to brave.

XV.

Day came; but on that soul no morning breaks
That does not dawn in hope—the day and night
Are but as one to him whom she forsakes:
The sun shines not for spirits reft of light!
His radiance, to that wretched father's sight,
Did but appear his misery to mock;
Leaving him dark when all around was bright;
Unconscious of his beams as the scath'd rock,
Unmov'd by melting noon, or tempest's fiery shock.

XVI.

The only tie for which he loved the world
Was snapt—snapt rudely by one cruel blow;
The living temple of his love was hurl'd
In sudden desolation—nought below
Remain'd, but one unbroken path of woe:
He did but live the prey of every thought
That wastes the springs of life—to feel and know
That earth, with all her scenes, to bim was nought,
Or but a cheerless waste, with grief and frenzy fraught.

XVII.

He now had but one thought the world to give—
He now had but one boon—life's last—to crave!
That thought—how long he was condemn'd to live—
That boon but this—a quickly yielded grave!
His last —sole joy he hoped no more to have :
Like one upon a lonely island thrown,
From whom the world has taken all it gave—
All, but what dying wretches make their own—
The freehold of the tomb—all else for ever flown.

XVIII.

He lived—breath'd—walk'd, like one of sense bereft!

He saw not—heard not, any living thing!

He seem'd a moving form that mind had left;

His consciousness, absorb'd in one wild sting,

Found not an object friend or foe could bring,

To rouse his spirit from its apathy!

He mutter'd to the wind; and seem'd to fling

His glance on air, as if he hoped to see

Some form embodied there, that lived in memory.

XIX.

He sat within his desolated room,

And gazed for hours on the unmoving door;

As watching for some form that might illume

His deep'ning darkness—but it came no more

To smile on him—its glance of light was o'er!

Then—sheets of lightning might have wrapp'd his
                    head—

And nearest thunders peal'd in loudest roar—

Nor rous'd him from that trance, so deep and dread—

By frequent start alone distinguish'd from the dead.

XX.

When the wild storm of rage and sorrow closes;
When the mind sinks into a listless state
Exhausted, and in living death reposes—
When nought can rouse its fear, nor love, nor hate—
'Tis then beheld most lost and desolate!
It shows the chords of feeling in that strain
Have burst; and the heart sunk beneath the weight
Of woe, from which it ne'er may rise again—
Curs'd even in the loss of wrath, and fear, and pain.

XXI.

Yes—there is life in anger and in sorrow—
The rage may cease—the tear be dried away—
The heart, though wrung to day, may thrill to-morrow;
The starting pulse resume its healthful play;
As night and cold are chas'd by warmth and day—
But when the soul, unmov'd by joy or woe,
Sinks listless—reckless in its shell of clay—
When neither sigh will heave, nor tear will flow;
Its state is hopeless then—it scarce will wake below.

· · XXII.

Some men have minds of such elastic power, ,
That there is scarce a grief can weigh them down;
They may be tortur'd—wrung—in sorrow's hour;
But rise they will, despite fate's darkest frown—
Others, by loss of fortune, friends, renown—
Seem crush'd as if they ne'er again could soar—
Few eyes have waked that tears could never drown;
Few hearts have beat that anguish never bore;
But each has some fine chord may shake it to its core.

XXIII.

And Leon—did he droop in grief at home?
No! he was wand'ring like a restless shade,
Doom'd for a penance round some spot to roam,
Where all it loved in life was mould'ring laid—
Where memory all its perish'd joys portray'd—
Nor peace by day, nor sleep by night he knew;
Reck'd not what ills he bore, nor where he stray'd;
Nor felt the rain that fell—the wind that blew—
So lost to all but one absorbing grief he grew.

XXIV.

Sometimes upon a precipice he lay,

That crumbled o'er a horrid gulph below!

But stirr'd not—shook not—fear was past away;

All but the stubbornness of desperate woe!

An earthquake heav'd the hills—he did not know

It had been there—unfelt by him it past!

Life—death—no worse than he had borne could show :

Upon the lake a frenzied look he cast,

As deeming there his love perchance had breath'd her last.

XXV.

He felt like exile on his prison rock;

Or felon on the morrow doom'd to die—

Whom the bright hues of nature do but mock

With cruel splendour; on the glowing sky

He look'd but with a thankless—desperate eye:

The very wind past by him with a groan!.

Night was the welcomest—then he might lie,

And vent his furious grief, unseen—alone—

Her starless darkness best accorded with his own.

H

XXVI.

If sleep would come—'twas but a fever'd dream—
His burning hands were clench'd in agony!
His wild and restless fancy did but teem
With shapes of horror—sights of misery!
Eva was ever there; and seem'd to be
The living, suffering spirit of each scene;
Now struggling with some ruthless enemy—
Then lifeless in her gore—as she had been
The victim of some crime, that fill'd that space between.

XXVII.

Then he would madly strain his eager grasp,
As if he hoped to snatch her from the grave—
Now felt her cold—now burning in his clasp—
Panting to succour—to avenge—or save—
He saw the phantom pass—and woke to rave!
Darkness was in his soul, and round his head—
No thought was left that light or promise gave;
The spring of youth—the glow of life, were fled;
And hideous, dark despair, its fatal influence shed.

XXVIII.

Reck'd it to one so lost that earth was green?
That fields, flowers, trees—blush'd in a flood of light?
For him there was no blessing in the scene—
Nature for others smiled, and heaven was bright—
He saw all blasted with a sudden blight!
His curse clung to him wheresoe'er he went;
And blacken'd what would else have blest his sight:
He look'd and felt like one whose heart was rent,
To find the hopes of life in one wide ruin blent.

XXIX.

Who knew him happy, scarce had known him then—
His cheek was deathly; dim and sunk his eye;
He seem'd a spectre in the paths of men—
As murderer shuns the morning, would he fly
The busy, smiling throng; where joy was nigh
His curse was doubled; and he felt alone
Far more, than when beneath the midnight sky
He stray'd; he would that none should hear him groan—
Since none could sooth his pangs, he wish'd them all
   unknown.

XXX.

It is no common sorrow that can turn,
To one dark theme, a mind that ranged o'er all—
And chill the ardent soul that erst did burn
With more than mortal fire; and ev'n inthral
The wings of fancy, till they close and fall;
Or bind a young heart to one changeless thought,
Till it is work'd to frenzy past recal!
Till the intense excitement, over-wrought,
Hath o'er the shaken mind, the rage of mania brought.

XXXI.

The lamp was glimmering in the Father's room;
And its dim ray, through that still chamber spread,
Gave only light enough to show the gloom—
A taper in a mansion of the dead!
What foot is that which moves with noiseless tread,
And steps as if it fear'd the floor might speak?—
Is it a foe that comes his blood to shed?
No! 'tis a form of love—it does but seek
To steal a last look there—and once more kiss that cheek.

XXXII.

'Tis Eva! does she fear a Father's eye ?
She who around him loved her arms to throw—
No—she but dreads to see its agony—
She trembles lest she wake him to his woe—
She deems him slumb'ring—ah ! she does not know
'Tis but the stupor of a spirit broken !
She would not cause his tears again to flow
For worlds—howe'er desiring one last token
Of his unalter'd love   whether 'twere look'd or spoken.

XXXIII.

She bends her o'er his couch with streaming eyes ;
She starts—she shrinks —as though she knew him not !
His alter'd features freeze her in surprize ;
As something scarce remember'd, nor forgot—
And—" Oh !" she cried—" what woe hath been thy lot,
To work so deep a change in such short space!
In those few days since last I saw this spot,
The bloom—the flesh hath almost left thy face ;
Where paths of scalding tears, in these deep tracks I trace.

XXXIV.

" Too well I see what agonies have wrung
Thy heart, to change thy features thus to sight ;
The hue of death sorrow hath o'er them flung,
And sudden turn'd these late dark tresses white :
Too soon the grave will pall them in its night—
I see the shaft hath sped—this is no sleep
To cheer the soul—'tis on the eve of flight !
Not many times these eyes will ope' to weep—
Not many hopeless nights of painful vigils keep !

XXXV,

But few days past—and I was happy here—
This form so lifeless now—then look'd and smiled ;
And thought and felt as there were nought to fear :
One star his path illumin'd and beguil'd—
It was his last—his only light—his child !
A cloud came o'er it, and 'twas lost for ever—
For him it left a dark and hopeless wild ;
It brought a storm that only burst to sever
His soul from light and life ; from whose dark void it never

XXXVI.

Can wake on earth again! why did I seek
, This sight of more than agony! to view
The hand of death upon so dear a cheek!
'Tis cold and damp with life's last ev'ning dew—
, And yet I wish'd to breathe one last adieu
Unheard—unseen to take one look—the last—
Of him round whom my soul's affection grew—
I long'd to clasp his hand ere life was past;
Then perish like the flower that falls beneath the blast."

XXXVII.

She stood some moments o'er him, breathing woe;
Full of the bitter thoughts of days gone by;
As one upon the verge of all below!
And from her breast there burst a long, deep sigh—
From sleep it might have rous'd him—but his eye
Exhaustion seal'd—she knelt—his hand she grasp'd—
A tear fell on it that she would not dry—
She gave her full soul vent—his neck she clasp'd—
And kiss'd his pale, parch'd lips; and shook, and
    sobb'd, and gasp'd!

XXXVIII.

And yet he did not rouse him from that trance;
There still was warmth, else she had deem'd him dead!
And he was all unconscious of the glance—
His Eva's glance—the tears his Eva shed!
Yet she was near him—saw him—touch'd him—bled
At heart, to see him petrifying there;
She with whom hope, joy, life and spirit, fled—
Whose loss alone had wrought that deep despair—
Was then beside his couch, his last of woe to share!

XXXIX.

She had design'd, unmark'd, to view his face;
With one unwitness'd look to sooth her heart:
(As some fond spirit comes unseen to trace
The form it loved in life)—and then depart—
She fear'd her presence would revive the smart—
But now to see him in that apathy,
Was worse than deepest sob, and wildest start;
That state of living death, and misery,
Whatever might befal, she could not bear to see.

XL.

She grasp'd him harder—wildly kiss'd his cheek!
And laid her burning face upon his neck—
The chamber echoed with a desperate shriek,
That fear no longer prompted her to check!
He roused a moment from his being's wreck—
Like a wild sun o'er an autumnal frost;
That yields, before it sinks, one last bright speck
Betwixt the clouds the storm hath round it tost—
Then drops in deeper shade, and is in darkness lost.

XLI.

He moved—he roll'd his wild and glassy eye
Upon the form that o'er him weeping bent—
Burst from his lips a strange and piercing cry,
Like maniacs utter when their souls are rent!
Where every tone of human voice seem'd blent—
There but escap'd his lips one thrilling word—
'Twas Eva's name—to Eva's soul it went!
Then backward on his couch he fell, nor stirr'd—
Nor sign of life was left—nor sound of breath was heard.

H 2

XLII.

She waited for another look—in vain—

His eyes were closed for ever—then she felt

His heart—'twas still—it knew not joy nor pain :

Kind fate the last and welcome blow had dealt ;

And freed the spirit that in torture dwelt.

She stood some moments in a frenzied woe,

Till her too conscious soul began to melt;

When sorrow's unrestrain'd and gushing flow,

Reliev'd her bursting heart, half broken by that blow.

XLIII.

She wept an hour beside him, nor once moved

Her eye from his unanswering, marble face :

Although that form, the first, last, most beloved—

Half blinded by her tears, she scarce could trace :

And Oh! what thoughts rush'd crowding in that space!

Years past in swift and agoniz'd review—

The many deeds of love—the look—th' embrace—

And the kind word in quick succession flew;

Making that hour a life, in thought, and feeling too.

XLIV.

She moved to leave him—but return'd again,·
To take another look ; to sob one more
Farewell, as if her heart, though wrench'd with pain,
Scarce wish'd that scene of suffering to be o'er—·
Thrice her limbs trembled—totter'd to the door—
As often she return'd again, to see
The last impression that those features bore ;
To grave them deeper in her memory—
Nay—ev'n to wake again those thoughts of agony.

XLV.

Hard is the parting, when the call of death
Has bidden some loved spirit take its flight—
But scarcely with the last departing breath,
Does the survivor feel forsaken quite ;
There still is something left to meet the sight—
The form is there, although the soul has sped—
But when the grave has pall'd it in its night—
Then—then we feel alone—for all is fled!
Then first we truly know what 'tis to mourn the dead.

XLVI.

She gave his hand her last—her farewell pressure—
'Twas clammy—cold—she felt she must—must go—
Yet hung like dying miser o'er his treasure,
About to pass from all he loved below.
Love, ev'n for things inanimate, may grow
From long acquaintance—how much more for those
Who lived affection's kindest proofs to show;
From whom to part for ever, seems to close
The door on hope, to leave life nothing but its woes.

XLVII.

To each loved spot she past she sigh'd farewell—
They were the scenes of happiness gone by :
A thousand silent objects seem'd to tell
Of past delights—whatever met her eye—
Her books—her harp—not useless wont to lie—
Her favourite bird, whose cage was now his tomb—
With her own desolation seem'd to vie !
Lone, dreary, silent, was each lifeless room ;
Save when her hurried steps rung hollow through the
    gloom.

XLVIII.

She left the place where every tie once bound her;
Her soul was in the deepest—last distress!
The night was dark—the wind clasp'd chilly round
    her;
The very air seem'd fraught with bitterness:
The world had nothing left to sooth or bless—
Save one fond, faithful being—he alone
Remain'd to cheer the hopeless—fatherless:
To answer every tear, and every groan;
To blend his grief with hers, and make her wrongs his
    own.

XLIX.

And he was as the star that led her on,
Amidst the blackness of that withering night;
When every other orb of heaven was gone:
With that she did not feel abandon'd quite—
And but for that despair had seal'd her sight—
So looks the seaman on the polar star,
When clouds have veil'd each other gem of light;
Whose solitary ray, that shoots afar,
May haply guide him through the elemental war.

L.

And did she seek to bless him with her love—
Him, next her sire, the being of her soul?
Far sterner passions now that youth must move—
Far fiercer looks than love's her eye must roll !
Revenge was rous'd, and raging past controul !
The sorrow that had torn her heart, was turn'd
To vengeance, and to wreak it was the goal
For which her chang'd and madden'd spirit burn'd ;
While every softer thought was from her bosom spurn'd.

LI.

Leon was stretch'd upon his couch, from sleep
As far as if amidst the battle's heat :
The thoughts that fill'd his mind were wild and deep—
His pulse was striking with a frenzied beat,
Till reason seem'd half shaken from her seat.
He would not—nay, he could not banish thence
The image of his Eva, though replete
With every anguish that can wring the sense
With sorrow and despair, devouring and intense.

LII.

There burst a well known voice upon his ear!
He scarcely hoped it from a mortal tongue—
It woke a thrill of mix'd surprize and fear—
He started—listen'd—and again it rung!
He dash'd his window open; and among
The trees his eye a cherish'd figure caught—
An instant past not, ere his arms were flung
Around the neck of Eva! every thought
With wonder and delight almost to frenzy wrought.

LIII.

Awhile she left him in his dream of joy—
She knew it was his last of happiness!
Her resolution falter'd to destroy
His bliss, whom nought, when that was past, could
    bless.
His kisses burning on her lips—nor less
The grasping pressure of his arms, declared
How vast his present joy—his past distress—
He wept in bliss to think that fate had spared
Her whom to meet on earth his soul had long despair'd.

LIV.

Yes—there are times when custom's fetters drop,
Even from souls the purest and the best;
When the warm gush of feeling will not stop,
For all the coldness of a virgin's breast;
When heart to heart, and lips to lips are prest—
But guiltless as the love of infancy!
When prudish eye, and censure half exprest,
Chill not, nor check the bosom's extacy;
When triumphs over all pure feeling's energy.

LV.

Such moments are when sorrow, joy, or fear,
Awake the uncurb'd spirit's native play;
When not a hand is rais'd to dash the tear,
That dims the eye it does not shame, away—
Such are when lovers meet, who, long the prey
Of absence, wept in wild and hopeless grief:
And well such moments do those pangs repay—
More welcome, since they are so few and brief:
Like sleep to pain, they bring a timely, sweet relief.

LVI.

Such moments then were Leon's ; while he held
The weeping fair one in his straining fold :
But O ! their breasts what different feelings swell'd ?
He saw not that her eye in frenzy roll'd—
He did not dream her heart was wrench'd and cold ;
The very home of life's complete despair !
He thought her agitated breathings told
That hope, and love, and rapture revell'd there—
And happy deem'd himself such strong regards to share.

LVII.

There past some moments, and they swiftly past,
Before the question came—" Where hast thou been ?
What hast thou suffer'd since I saw thee last—
What mystery hath work'd those days between ?
To tear thee from thy friends—thy home—the scene
Of all thy joys—to wring thy father's breast,
And mine, with fears so wild, and pangs so keen—?
O ! tell me, that suspense may sink to rest ;
And joy awake again ; and love pronounce us blest !"

LVIII.

"Leon! I do not come to talk of love—
Vengeance demands those hours that else were sweet!
I come thy courage and thy faith to prove—
Nay—nay—I doubt them not—nor need entreat
Thy arm to right me; for thy heart will beat
With fury and with hate as deep as mine—
Thy soul will burn for vengeance as complete
As I would launch, had I a hand divine!
If mine the grief and shame—the wrong is also thine!

LIX.

"I left my Father on his bed of death—
One blow has smitten him, and me, and thee!
My burning lips receiv'd his parting breath;
And I was in the depth of misery!
And yet—tis best he did not live to see—
To hear my wrong; without avail to mourn
A daughter's hopeless, cureless injury;
Outliving peace—hope—honor—and to burn
That happiness to feel, that never could return.

LX.

"A villain seiz'd me—brutal strength prevail'd—
I had no dagger, and my hand was weak!
He found me in the ruins—there, assail'd
By force, I suffer'd—what, were I to speak,
The burning blushes would consume my cheek!
I had no lightnings in my frenzied eye—
There were no thunders in my desperate shriek—
What now remains but to avenge and die;
Since sunder'd from the earth is every cherish'd tie?

LXI.

"But I escaped—for though I felt that life
Was blasted, and had nought but bitterness;
Nor more could hope the joys of mother, wife—
A wrong'd and broken heart, like mine could bless—
And though I wish'd to die—what could I less—
I would not—could not—ere I saw the wretch,
Whose ruffian guilt had stabb'd my happiness—
Beneath the sword of justice—vengeance—stretch—
And his last lab'ring breath in gasping anguish fetch."

LXII.

And Leon seem'd as wrath had stopt his breath !
His bosom like a pent volcano heav'd—
His cheeks—his lips, became as white as death—
Fierce as a Lion, of his mate bereav'd,
Turns on the hunter who her fall achiev'd;
So did he burn for vengeance on his head,
Whose work of woe could never be retriev'd !
Whom, if a curse could kill, it had not sped,
So ardently he wish'd himself his blood to shed.

LXIII.

But when he look'd upon that lovely form,
Bent as in shame, and withering in her woe;
And smitten like a lily in the storm;
O'er his fierce passion pity seem'd to throw
Her soft'ning influence—tears began to flow—
He strain'd her to his sympathizing heart;
Whispering that peace himself could never know;
And striving, with affection's kindest art,
To heal—if ought could heal, her deep-wrung spirit's
     smart.

LXIV.

It did shed comfort on her soul to find,
Who loved her happy—loved her now no less—
That he, despite of ruin, still was kind,
As in her days of hope and joyfulness !
But most it pierc'd her that she could not bless
A being so unalterably true;
That one so valued, she could ne'er possess ;
And o'er the darkness of her thoughts it threw
A more entire despair—and clouds of blacker hue.

LXV.

" Thou talk'st of dying—No ! my Eva, live—
To know my vengeance was complete—severe—
What peace life yet hath left, 'tis mine to give :
Mine though thou canst not be, we may be dear—
Dear to each other still—mix tear with tear,
In some unbroken, dreary solitude ;
There, far from mortal eye, and mortal ear,
We still may sooth each other, though we brood
On grief, until we find e'en joy in that dark mood.

LXVI.

" But tell me now—where does this fiend abide?
For he and I breathe not another day!
Do thou to his accursed presence guide—
And one or both, the sword shall surely slay.
Nor food, nor sleep, shall cheer, till I obey
This paramount command! I hold my life
But as devoted to this deadly fray—
Whichever heaven may destine to the knife,
It is not ours to tell—'tis mine to seek the strife.

LXVII.

" 'Tis sure we do not meet as common foes;
One sword shall be the messenger of fate:
Once met—we do not part till death shall close
The eyes of one for ever! such a hate
No doom, while pulse remain'd to beat, could sate:
If life's last drop in anguish be not drain'd;
The smarting wounds—the pangs however great—
All—all were nought! If life—if hope remain'd—
Revenge's burning wish would be but half attain'd."

LXVIII.

She spake—" Thou know'st the ruins—where we
    changed,
If not the sweetest looks of love, the first :
That scene, where oft' in innocence we ranged,
Became to me the blackest and the worst—
'Twas there the villain—be his soul accurst!
No pitying heart—no helping arm were near—
On the black walls my cries unheeded burst!
O ! had they reach'd a sire's or lover's ear ;
They had not rung in vain, nor I had ought to fear."

LXIX.

The night was more than dark—and the clouds drew
Together in their blackness : wild and dread
At intervals the fiery tempest flew ;
And rending midnight's sable mantle, shed
A transient, awful light ; the thunder spread
Its deep reverberating roll around :
Broad sheets of lightning flash'd above the head,
Reaching at once from heaven to the ground :
Then vanish'd but to leave more dark night's dread
    profound.

LXX.

They started not, nor trembled, at the roar;
And when the lightning wrapt them in its flame,
Though standing in its flash, they felt no more
Than if the kindest beams of morning came:
Had nature smiled, their thoughts had been the same;
Their inward anguish mock'd all outward ill:
An earthquake might have shaken nature's frame;
And the unbridled sea o'er plain and hill
Roll'd deluging—their souls no fiercer pangs could
    fill.

LXXI.

Full scope had they within for every thought—
She bore the wrong that woman feels the most;
That leaves a virtuous soul to madness wrought!
That dooms peace, honor, hope, for ever lost;
And frame and spirit in one ruin tost:
That stamps a stain no time can wear away;
That sheds a woe, sighs, tears can ne'er exhaust;
A keen regret, that sharpens day by day;
Till of those blended pangs ev'n life becomes the prey.

LXXII.

And if there be an injury that can wake
The breast of man to more than mortal ire;
And from his soul all feeling, pity, shake;
And light revenge and hatred's fiercest fire—
And if there be a wrong that could inspire
His hand a brother's—father's blood to shed—
That wrong was Leon's—and his wrath was dire!
Love check'd or thwarted has to slaughter led;
But blasted thus would crave to torture ev'n the dead.

LXXIII.

Were it a demon who had shed the blood
Of all he loved on earth, and 'midst their gore
Before his harrow'd sight exulting stood;
His spirit could not thirst for vengeance more!
Life has no deeper hate than what he bore!
Robb'd of his destin'd bride in all her bloom—
Dash'd from the hope that nothing could restore
From its untimely—unexpected tomb—
And love and all its sweets buried in one black doom.

LXXIV.

They tarried not, nor hasten'd, for the storm
But past like troubled spirits o'er the ground,
Who sped some deed of darkness to perform :
Like guilty things they travers'd night's profound ;
They reach'd th' ascent on which those ruins frown'd;
They heard the murmur of the waters dashing,
Breaking the silence that prevail'd around ;
Save when the thunder broke in awful crashing ;
And the wind's sudden gust the rising waves was lashing.

LXXV.

From one dark tower there broke a feeble light ;
Like Mars' red beam through midnight's murky air :
Soon as its ray had flash'd on Eva's sight,
She started—shriek'd—and cried—" The wretch is
    there !
I know it by the torch's wavering glare !
Ev'n now perchance he seeks me in that tower—
Be it his scene of horror and despair !
There may he perish ere another hour ;
And more than death's worst pangs his ruthless heart
    devour."

LXXVI.

Like Tiger scenting prey, when Leon knew
He was so near the presence of his foe;
Forward with swift and sudden bound he flew;
His spirit burning to inflict the blow;
And thirsting for that heart's last drop to flow.
With lightning's speed he swept the steep ascent—
He could as soon have staid for morn to show
Its golden beam, as cull the path he went,
Where rock nor yawning gulph his progress could
    prevent.

LXXVII.

Eva o'ertook him in the outer court;
The weakness—softness—of her sex she spurn'd:
Her native energy could still support,
Though now 'twas all to hate and fury turn'd:
Within those walls the direst passions burn'd
That can a wrong'd and desperate bosom tear—
Within their fatal precincts first she learn'd
What depth of crime a guilty soul can dare;
How man can glut on woe and revel o'er despair!

LXXVIII.

The warmest—brightest scenes that earth can show;
Oft' see the tempest's wildest fury flung;
The noblest—kindest hearts that beat below,
By wrongs unmerited, to madness wrung,
Are oft' the deadliest when too deeply stung!
As if all but their strength had past away—
The generous feelings that around them clung,
Seem changed to deep, dark passions, whose fierce
     sway
Might sear the softest heart, and make it joy to slay.

LXXIX.

And Eva—she who ne'er could hear, nor see
The plaint—the woe—but what she shared and felt—
She who could scarcely dream of misery,
But her whole soul would into pity melt;
In her changed breast now found that fury dwelt,
And thirsting vengeance; joy'd she could have stood
To see in that foe's heart the death-blow dealt;
And steel'd by wrongs, had smiled to see his blood
Spread round her very feet its red and stiff'ning flood.

LXXX.

They stopp'd for breath—they heard him pace the
 room,
Muttering deep curses at his victim's flight—
Instant the door was shiver'd; and the gloom
Of one pale lamp reveal'd him to the sight!
His figure was of broad and towering height;
A sable plume his lofty brow o'ershaded;
He seem'd a demon stalking through the night!
A momentary fear his breast pervaded;
When, starting, he beheld his solitude invaded.

LXXXI.

Rolling a glance of stern and black defiance,
His sword was in an instant bared to view;
For well he knew it was his sole reliance:
Like answer Leon gave him, for he drew,
And sent a look of such dark, deadly hue,—
If look could blast, one soul had perish'd there!
Had then an angel interposed to sue;
For mercy—pardon—pray'd him to forbear—
The boon had been refused—that man he would not spare.

LXXXII.

And Leon held no parley with that foe;
He sought him not to wage a war of speech:
The look he sent was follow'd by the blow,
And mortal fury nerv'd the arm of each;
The single aim who first the heart might reach—
It was not pride, nor glory, that inspired;
Interminable hatred form'd the breach—
The fiercest vengeance man can cherish fired;
And nothing short of death to sate its thirst desired.

LXXXIII.

Fast flash'd their swords, and heavily they fell;
Though Leon in such wrath could scarce be cool;
Yet still he knew to wield his weapon well:
His adversary, taught in discord's school,
Was not a foe the best might ridicule;
But Leon's eye and arm were quick as thought—
Though hard he found the task to overrule
The rage with which his panting breast was fraught,
Still every blow that came, his ready weapon caught.

LXXXIV.

The floor was shaken by their heavy tread;
And the walls echoed with the iron clash;
The wavering light the lamp around them shed,
Gleam'd from the steel, like lightning's distant flash—
The ruffian seem'd his very teeth to gnash
At the successless efforts of his ire;
While his life-blood flow'd fast from many a gash:
Their breath seem'd rushing from their lips in fire,
As in that lengthen'd strife their vengeance grew more
      dire.

LXXXV.

But Leon, as his foe exhausted grew,
Gather'd from hope new strength of limb and mind,
Instant with one deep thrust his sword past through,
And fix'd him writhing 'gainst the wall behind :
His head upon his bleeding breast reclined ;
His heart was sever'd, and his weapon fell;
Anguish of body—wrath of soul, combined
To make his dying scene the type of hell ;
Entwined and crush'd at last in evil's fatal spell.

LXXXVI.

Stretch'd on the bloody floor his pond'rous, length;
Death's pallid cloud crept slowly o'er his cheek;
Though the red stream had drain'd his limbs of strength,
He look'd the rage he had not power to wreak—
He tried to leave a curse—but could not speak!
One deep but momentary flush there past
Across his face—'twas like the wild red streak
Of setting sun, when storms are round it cast;
'Twas passion's wrathful close, that flash'd in death its
    last.

LXXXVII.

As the fierce Indian, when some snake has bitten
His best belov'd, his young and destin'd bride,
Looks on the reptile that his arm has smitten,
And sees it rolling, writhing by his side—
His wrath not in its death half satisfied—
So Leon o'er his lifeless victim stood;
His vengeance scarcely sated, though he died:
He could have crush'd the carcass in its blood;
Embedded as it lay in its once vital flood.

LXXXVIII.

Eva, pale, trembling, had beheld the strife,

Fearful lest vengeance might not be complete;

And more than anxious for her lover's life—

But when she saw his enemy retreat,

And fall, and gasp, and stiffen at his feet—

She had no further wish, nor object, left:

Save quickly life's last welcome throb to meet—

Of all that could her being bless bereft,

Ah! what was life to her with heart so deeply cleft!

LXXXIX.

As Leon stood, wrapt, gazing on his foe,

As though he wish'd to wake him from the dead;

To pierce—to rend him with another blow;

Until his ruthless soul again had fled—

He heard her fall—he started—saw she bled!

The fatal dagger in her hand was grasp'd:

Too late he flew—he rais'd her throbbing head—

Her bleeding bosom to his own he clasp'd,

And as he prest it there but felt how quick it gasp'd.

XC.

Deep sorrow choked the words he would have spoken;
He could but gaze, and groan in agony;
His thoughts were frenzied—wild—his heart seem'd
    broken,
To feel her growing colder; and to see
Her life in that red gushing torrent flee;
Another hour she would be gone for ever—
And he the prey of lonely misery!
Perchance one minute more—and he could never
Behold that living form, from which 'twas woe to sever.

XCI.

He had just look'd on death so pitiless,
It might be thought his soul was void of feeling—
But when he view'd her dying loveliness,
From whom the vital stream was swiftly stealing,
His thrilling brain in agony was reeling!
He saw the dews of death o'erspread her face—
The liquid light within her eyes congealing;
Till their late heavenly blue he scarce could trace,
Through the pale mists of death, that came their beams
    to chase.

XCII.

Long as her orbs the living spark possess'd,
Their souls seem'd beaming from each other's eyes—
Long as her heart had motion in her breast,
They spoke their grief—'twas all they could—in
    sighs !
In such a scene the look at once supplies
The loss of language—words are all too weak
To paint the frenzied feelings there that rise—
'Tis the eye's question, and the answering cheek—
'Tis these alone can tell what lips could scarcely speak :

XCIII.

And well they understood them; nor had need
Of words, their thoughts—their feelings to explain—
And though he mourn'd, he scarce could blame the
    deed ;
He felt—he own'd—she never could regain
The hope that she was dash'd from ; nor obtain
The restitution of her joy—her fame :
What choice was left her, but to burst the chain
That bound her to a life of grief and shame—
Or perish by degrees beneath a blasted name?

XCIV.

He, agonized, knelt leaning over her—
She fondly turn'd her closing eyes on him—
Wrapt in each other, neither seem'd to stir;
But she was dying fast—th' exhausted limb
Sunk ne'er to rise again! Her sight grew dim;
And death was fixing her last look in stone!
Her head fell back—her senses seem'd to swim—
The ling'ring life was smitten from its throne;
And consciousness expired in one faint—faultering
    groan.

XCV.

And life's last pang was past—the opal spark
That shone within her eye, was quench'd in night—
That animated eye was soulless—dark—
Like an extinguished star in heaven's blue light:
Gone was the magic smile that charm'd the sight!
That mind of more than female energy,
Had taken its irrevocable flight:
That perfect form—those limbs of symmetry—
Fix'd in the sunless frost of death's cold statuary.

XCVI.

A moment past—there was a being there,
On whom his happiness, his hopes depended—
And now he is alone, and in despair ;
And every feeling that he cherish'd ended—
A moment past, their looks, their sighs were blended ;
And now there does but lie a lifeless thing—
A corse upon its bed of blood extended ;
That can no longer share, nor know, the sting
That recollection leaves, his sever'd heart to wring.

XCVII.

She, young and fair, and in the bud of life,
Had cut its thread and leapt into the tomb—
While thousands shrink, and tremble at the knife ;
And cling enamour'd to a wretch's doom ;
In age, pain, poverty, and dungeon's gloom ;
Cherishing to the last life's fluttering flame ;
Though anguish, want, despair, and wrongs consume,
They fasten still to earth, in grief or shame ;
And dread at last to quit a wrung and wither'd frame.

XCVIII.

In one short hour how much had Leon borne !
His lost love found—but found in misery—
Fond hopes revived, to be as quickly torn—
A tale of horror heard in agony !
A mortal fight—a slaughter'd enemy—
The dying scene of her whose bliss he sought—
These in that space had past so suddenly ;
It might be thought some troubl'd dream had wrought
Its wild creations there, with fear and horror fraught.

XCIX.

With folded arms, and looks of fix'd despair,
He views the form where still affection clings :
Th' unwelcome beam of morning finds him there—
Is it because the sorceress, Memory, flings
Her circle round, he bears her thousand stings ;
And moves not—looks not—from that sight of woe !
He will not quit it, though it wake the springs
Of all the sharpest sorrows man can know,
And force the deepest sighs that e'er he heaves below.

C.

That was the form which in its life return'd
A love as pure as mortal heart e'er felt—
Those were the lips, and that the breast, that burn'd;
And those the eyes that made his spirit melt—
In whose blue softness fascination dwelt—
Now they are nothing—yet he would not leave them,
Till fate its last remaining blow had dealt;
And that was when he saw the earth receive them ;
When tears his burning eyes might visit—and relieve
    them.

CI.

As pure a heart as ever throbb'd with life,
Was there lain lonely in its narrow rest ;
Beyond the further reach of pain or strife—
As fair a form as earth's green couch e'er prest,
There slept, and wild-flowers bloom'd above her breast :
There the night-winds in mournful dirges swept ;
And there, with all-devouring grief possest,
When all was dark around him, Leon crept—
Nor saw—nor thought of aught—save her for whom he
    wept.

CII.

How soon the scene of human bliss is wreck'd :
Heaven sends the bolt—the loved ones drop away!
Each lives to bear what none could once expect—
Fond hearts of sever'd feelings fall the prey!
Friends perish—parted—scatter'd in dismay!
One day gave Sire and Daughter to the grave—
And e'er another shed its noontide ray,
It saw the lover bounding o'er the wave;
Reckless if rode his bark, or sunk where none could
    save.

END OF EVA.

ELECTRICITY.

———

WRITTEN FOR THE FIFTEENTH ANNIVERSARY OF
THE PHILOMATHIC INSTITUTION; 1822.

ELECTRICITY.

MAN lives in wonders: wheresoe'er he moves,
Her mystic powers unerring Nature proves:
The seas that waft him, and the earth he treads;
The air that round its vital influence sheds;
Each hath its miracles, and all proclaim
Th' unseen Omnipotent from whom they came.
On every side enchantment meets the view,
From earth's dark depths, through heaven's vast arch
    of blue;
Myst'ries that science, toiling to explore,
Does but unfold to lead the way to more;
And can but prove, when life's short sand is run,
That human learning scarcely is begun.

'Tis not for man to trace the magic maze
Of Nature, in her deep and hidden ways;
Nor is it giv'n to finite sense to know
The infinite intelligence below.
To Him alone, who earth and heaven hath made,
The secrets of creation stand display'd.
When the wild storm that blackens all the sky,
Gathers in wrath and bids its terrors fly—
Unchains the thunders—hurls them through the air,
And shoots around the lightning's startling glare—
What bids those potent elements arise,
To mix in rage, and battle in the skies?
When the tornado whirls around the plain,
And leaves towns wreck'd, and men and cattle slain;
Who can resolve the reason of that strife,
That bids the air we breathe make war on life?
Or when the earthquake heaves, and cities fall,
And desolation seems to threaten all;
When mountains reel, and sever from their base,
Or sinking leave a flood to mark their place;
And plains are rent, and hideous gulphs appear,
Whence horrid sounds come rushing on the ear;
Down whose dark depths the shrieking victims go,
And living find an undigg'd grave below—

Where is the tongue, of earthly mould, shall tell
What makes the solid ground to shake and swell;
What nether power uplifts th' enormous weight
Of earth and stone that seem as fix'd as fate !
Who knows how deep the brooding mischiefs lurk—
What sets the boiling elements at work ?
Seeming at times from realm to realm to go,
As if continuous caverns stretch'd below;
Where struggling tempests, pent in darkness, sweep,
To ravage nations, and convulse the deep !
And still more wond'rous who can yet explain,
Why points the needle northward o'er the main ?
Whether the heavens be bright or dark above—
Whate'er the point from which the winds may move ;
Whether the ocean billows gently sweep—
Or horror stride the bosom of the deep—
The faithful compass fails not, night nor day,
To guide the seaman on his pathless way ;
And points the track, that none without could tell,
Back to the native shores he loves so well.
And him benighted in Columbia's woods ;
Wilder'd midst trackless wastes, or inland floods;
However far the chase may tempt to roam ;
His guardian Angel, still it leads him home ;

Who else perchance would perish in the wild;
Nor more return to clasp his wife or child.
Mysterious power! with more than magic fraught!
Passing the utmost search of human thought!
Inexplicable influence—that so far
Still draws the magnet towards the polar star:
As if two distant spirits converse held;
Whose mingling thoughts at once each bosom swell'd.
Is it some subtle fluid, that unseen
Extends the magnet and the pole between;
And stretching ev'n to earth's remotest shore,
Exists where land is found or surges roar?
Nor less th' Electric power pervades around;
Present wherever vital air is found:
Circling this ample globe in all its pride;
Unfelt—unseen--though spread on every side;
Save when the lightning meets the startled sight,
Or meteors sporting rend the veil of night;
Piercing the very ground on which we tread;
Charging the clouds that darken over head—
Now silent gleaming, like a falling star,
As if some orb had left its path afar;
Now flashing for an instant on the eye—
Then lost amidst the darkness of the sky!

As though some spirit, on its airy flight,

Had shot on wings of flame across the night;

Or blazing serpent, not for hope display'd,

Impell'd its fiery form amidst the shade.

What time—what place—in which it is not found,

If the glass cylinder be whirl'd around?

Snapping and sparkling as it gathers there,

Brought to a focus from the circling air;

And if in darkness drawn, it meets the view,

In one continued stream of vivid hue—

Until concentrated its power to show,

It staggers manhood with the sudden blow!

And almost seems, if such the deadly will—

Potent enough the pulse of life to still.

Lo! in the darken'd room, its sparkling rays

Proclaim its presence to the wond'ring gaze;

The mimic lightning, sporting on the view,

At man's desire reveals its dazzling hue;

As though the elements were in his hand,

And nature ev'n acknowledg'd his command.

Oft as excitement calls its mystic light,

It seems to start from nothing on the sight;

Flies swift as thought around its wiry path;

Potent but harmless—lightning without wrath!

In fiery forms it flashes on the eye;
As if by magic summon'd from the sky—
The blazing shafts of death innoxious play,
And gently strike, or hurtless die away:
For ever present, yet but seldom seen,
It sports our lips and every breath between;
Circling at noon round our unconscious heads—
Passing at midnight by our silent beds—
A spirit, seldom tangible to sight,
To whom not oft is giv'n the power to smite;
Like a destroying Angel, passing by,
Sparing the form that it might doom to die;
The bolts of fate, though ready in its hand,
Not to be launch'd but by divine command.

This mystic force—to beasts—to man denied,
Th' Allwise hath given to forms that swim the tide;
That seem, though whelm'd in ocean's waves, to share
A portion of that power that cleaves the air:
And though they shed no lightning through the deep,
Their shocks benumbing o'er the vitals creep.
There the Torpedo, conscious of its might,
Prepares its force the hostile arm to smite;
And the advent'rous hand its touch that braves,

Recoils as from a foe beneath the waves.

And still more potent, where through wood and plain,

Columbia's giant rivers seek the main ;

Th' Electric eel displays its deadly form,

Arm'd with the vengeance of the thunder storm !

As it had drawn the lightning from the air,

Beneath the flood, to point destruction there :

Man from its withering touch starts back dismay'd ;

Nor scarcely dares its liquid haunt invade :

Through every nerve the deadening influence flies,

And momentary darkness clouds the eyes.

The scaly victims that it dooms its prey,

Scarce feel the blow ere life is dash'd away—

A very Basilisk beneath the tide,

Its look alone spreads death on every side.

Swift as the sun-beams reach the eastern hills,

When Sol th' awaken'd earth with glory fills ;

So darts th' electric fluid on its course,

With speed unrivall'd, and resistless force.

The lapse of time scarce human sense can mark,

That serves the distant transit of the spark ;

The measured moment scarcely is begun,

Before the flight that past o'er leagues is done !

K

Defying time—disowning even space—
It conquers both in its unrivall'd race!
In its velocity it leaves behind
The very thought that flashes through the mind;
And seems as it would reach the farthest star,
Before the mind could aim a flight so far.

  Lo! where the mingling clouds of lilac hue,
Gather above, and hide the sun from view ;
At first a deep'ning vapour seems to form,
The silent prophet of the coming storm;
Its lower surface flat, but arch'd above ;
Towards which the lighter clouds attracted move ;
Like flakes of wool, in fleecy form arranged,
And oft' in figure as in motion changed ;
At times uniting, and at times repell'd ;
Till to a giant mass the whole is swell'd ;
Seeming to move in wrath, as if it felt
The slumb'ring force that in its darkness dwelt !
And parting oft' to let the lurid light,
In fitful gleams shoot wildly on the sight ;
Tinged with the colour of the fev'rish clouds,
In whose dark bulk the brooding tempest shrouds ;
Onward they roll, full charged, in hostile rush—

Then, meeting—burst with that tremendous crash!
The sudden lightning flashing on the eye,
In one vast sheet of flame involves the sky;
At midnight seen, it shames the brightest moon,
And for an instant sheds a fearful noon;
Clothes all the plain in light; illumes the wood;
And in a fiery mantle wraps the flood.
Soon as the wide extended blaze has sped,
The thunder-crash bursts awful o'er the head,
Rolls in reverberating peals of sound,
And dies in distant echoes far around.
The beasts within their coverts disappear,
And birds fly screaming to their nests in fear.
Silence succeeds—an interval of dread!
Till farther off again the rage is shed;
Still leaving, as it seeks some distant shore,
A longer lapse betwixt the flash and roar;
Till the faint lightning scarce affects the eye;
And rumbling low the distant thunders die.

When bursts this elemental wrath above,
Scarce from his den the savage dares to move;
Thunder he deems the angry voice of God;
And in the lightning dreads his fiery rod!

While coward superstition starts with fear,

And thinks it ominous of evil near.

Far different thought had he,* that self-taught sage,

Columbia's pride, the wisest of his age ;

The first to soar with scientific mind,

The cause of that aërial strife to find.

With daring aim he rais'd th' Electric kite,

And brought the fluid down reveal'd to sight,

And proved that active and mysterious flame,

The muse's theme, and lightning but the same:

Thus nature's secret ways, if science scan,

Her wonders yet may reach the eye of man.

But let not him of less experience, dare

To draw its fiery arrows from the air ;

Lest from his heedless hand the shaft of death

Strike to his heart, and stop the vital breath.

Nor let the traveller, when the storm is fierce,

When through the dripping leaves the lightning

    pierce,

Let him not seek, where tow'rs the spreading tree,

For shelter to its treacherous shade to flee ;

For thither oft' attracted in its course,

In one destructive stroke it spends its force;

             * Dr. Franklin.

And leaves the blacken'd corse the tale to tell,
Of him who there had safety sought and fell.
Nor let the wanderer who beholds its beam,
Venture his steps beside the glassy stream;
Rivers and brooks conduct it on its way—
Unquench'd its fires along the waters play—
As if the very floods, with all their might,
Had not the power to check its burning flight:
Nor let him refuge seek, where the high wall
Offers a shelter from the rains that fall;
'Tis but a trait'rous friend, that leads the foe
From its high path, to smite the ground below;
And makes it turn and spend its fury there,
That harmless else might have dispers'd in air.
Nor should he fail to fly the fatal spark,
When just above his head the clouds grow dark;
Where its collecting force prepares to burst,
And dart strait down, in double-flash, its worst!
Then is it time to flee—if time be left—
Before the bolt the thread of life has reft:
Before the rosy cheek, and healthful form,
Lie blanch'd and cold, and stiff'ning in the storm.
And Oh! has fate a death so dread—so dire!
As thus to wither in this fatal fire?

Life closed at once—'midst all its hopes and fears—
Perchance while picturing future blissful years :
Even while fancy paints some dear delight;
Dash'd down for ever as it springs to sight!
Affections sundered in their fondest dream—
A midnight shot across noon's brightest beam—
Cut off unwarn'd, whether the passing thought
Be in a mood of good or evil wrought—
That thought itself unfinish'd, as it past
Across the mind that dream'd not of its last :
Hurried at once before the Judge of all—
Unthinking of th' irrevocable call :
No time allow'd to pour one instant prayer,
To plead beforehand for the guilty there ;
No crime confess'd to smooth the path to peace ;
That joy might waken, or despondence cease :
No moment given to breathe one swift farewell
To all those kindred beings loved so well—
To send one wish—the last—and from the heart—
To those from whom 'twas worse than death to part !
The thousand ties that link the soul below,
Annihilated by one instant blow :
Denied whate'er might sooth the bed of death,
And mingle comfort with the latest breath :

But in the twinkling of an eye to be
Living—a corse—and in eternity.
In days of Heathen darkness thus to die
Consign'd the corse untouch'd—untomb'd to lie;
Fenced round as if abhorrent to the sight,
Tempting the vulture from his lofty flight;
Bereft of all the honors of the dead;
To them, far more than death, a source of dread.
Deeming that Jupiter his bolt had hurl'd,
To smite in wrath th' accursed from the world,
Friends left his bones to whiten where they fell;
And fear'd to drop one tear, or sigh farewell.

Ah! happy he, who thus from being dash'd —
Whose spirit parted as the lightning flash'd—
Thrice happy he, who in his early days,
Had sought religion's safe and pleasant ways:
Who made his peace with heaven while life was spared,
Nor braved its bolt of vengeance unprepared;
Nor risk'd, since being hangs but on a thread,
With life's last step the paths of guilt to tread.
For him the flash, with all its deadly ire,
Is but Elijah's chariot of fire!
The peal that calls him hence—the flaming rod—

But leave him in the bosom of his God !
Released from all the ling'ring woe of death—
The fears the best may feel with life's last breath :
Spared all the pangs the soul must bear to part
From those whose love was twined about the heart;
Whose fondness still would strive, in hope or fear—
In pain or bliss—to chain the spirit here ;
When he, expiring, turns his eyes on those
He dreads will sink in anguish when they close—
Assured those hands that clasp his throbbing head,
Will wring in torture when his soul has fled.
But ah ! how few, in all this scene of strife,
Would chuse this sudden—awful close of life !
How few prepare to meet that instant call,
That heaven can make the lot of each—of all ;
How few would dare to ask it as a boon—
How few to whom it would not come too soon !

Lightning ! thou mystic element—unseen,
Save when thou flashest earth and heaven between ;
Where do thy hidden fires in ambush lie,
Ready to open on the startled eye ?
Tremendous power ! Omnipotent to slay !
A fiery demon bursting on the day—

Or blazing out amidst the shades of night,
Dispelling slumber from the shrinking sight.
Ere on the ear thy sudden death-peal roll—
Thy bolt hath from thy victim rent the soul!
None but the Deity could form thy reign—
His mighty hand alone thy shafts restrain.
Thy secret weapon rends the giant oak;
The sever'd steeple reels beneath thy stroke;
And smitten from its pride, and place on high,
Falls with tremendous crash in wreck to lie.
Kindled by thee the thirsty woods expire;
And the dark forest glows a sea of fire:
Thy blind, unsparing vengeance, seems to strike
The holy fane, and guilty haunt alike:
Now smites the altar—now the bed of crime—
And now the virtuous soul in being's prime
There instant falls the stiffen'd steed to die;
And here the blacken'd limbs of childhood lie.
What means, amidst the darkness of the night,
That sudden blaze that bursts upon the sight!
Thy flash hath reach'd the cot in its repose,
And in th' insatiate element it glows;
Its inmates buried in its burning tomb,
Or waking find but time to shun that doom;

And gazing on the flames in wild despair,
See their last hopes—their all—expiring there.

Lo! where the traveller treads his joyous way,
Enraptured with the various charms of day;
Dreaming no ill, he casts his eyes around,
To mark the beauties of the verdant ground;
Nor e'er conceives the thought that even then,
He looks his last on heaven, and earth, and men.
Sudden a tempest gathers o'er his head—
The boding clouds prepare their wrath to shed—
The flash envelopes him—a sudden pain,
Shoots swift as thought through every trembling vein!
He shrinks—he staggers—stretches forth his arms—
And seems an instant lost in dread alarms!
Too soon the frightful truth appals his soul;
And deep despair o'erwhelms him past controul—
He tries to strain his eyes—their orbs are dark!
That stroke for ever quench'd their optic spark!
For him no more shall rise the morning light;
For him no more the moon illume the night;
Beauty, which once he view'd with joy intense,
For him no more shall charm that best—lost sense:
Nor smile of friend shall cheer—nor looks of love

From his benighted soul one pang remove :
Nor crimson clouds shall glow, nor vallies bloom—
Henceforth his life is night—his home a tomb !
Fated to mourn till death in vain regret,
That first—best sense, he never can forget.

And who can tell, in nature's mystic ways,
What secret part this hidden fluid plays ;
What purpose the Unfathomable Mind,
From its pervading influence design'd ?
'Twas scarcely form'd alone to rend the air,
Though thunders speak it in commotion there—
Not merely sent to sport upon the eye,
When meteors point its presence in the sky ;
Nor launch'd in wrath the seat of life to smite ;
Nor quench the optic nerve in hopeless night.
A kinder—nobler end, decreed its birth ;
Alike perchance a friend to man and earth ;
Performing equally in rest or strife,
Some function needful for the springs of life.
Pomona's treasures ripen in its power;
And Flora owns its influence on the flower :
The garden all its secret impulse feels ;
And brighter charms, and richer fruit reveals :

Its vivifying essence spreads below—
Earth seems to ripen in its vital glow—
Till all the vegetable world displays
Its full perfection to th' admiring gaze.
Drawn from the clouds by nature, or by art,
It acts alike this fructifying part ;
Where thunder-rods invite it from the sky,
Or trees gigantic point their boughs on high,
A richer vegetation seems to spread,
As if another sun its influence shed.
Perchance as needful as the vital breath,
Without its spirit all might sink in death;
Since He who pour'd it through the realms of light,
Ne'er shows in vain his wisdom nor his might.

All-potent power! pervading earth and heaven !
To whom Omnipotence such sway hath given!
Present alike when angry tempests lour,
Or summer evening yields its tranquil hour ;
When silent lightning opens on the eye,
And thunder seems to slumber in the sky;
As if thy wrath, that sported in the air,
In mercy chain'd its bolts of vengeance there.
Alike in calm or storm for ever near ;

Type of thy Maker, omnipresent here.

Whether o'er sea or land the tempest roll;

Above the burning line, or frozen pole;

Whether it wrap in flame the mountain's crest,

Or bursting scare the peaceful vale from rest—

The spirit of the storm, thou still art there,

Enthron'd in clouds—the monarch of the air!

When tranquil, ever from our sight conceal'd,

And only in thy sport or wrath reveal'd.

When the Volcano pours its sea of fire;

And earth and heaven are crimson'd by its ire;

Thy vivid flash is seen above the rest;

Thy vollied peals roll round its blazing crest;

As if thy power had call'd its fury up,

And fill'd to overflow its fiery cup;

Or bursting from confinement in its womb,

Sprang forth in terrors from that burning tomb.

Nor art thou idle when the earthquake throws

Hills, plains, and cities, from their still repose:

Full charg'd with thee, the hot and stagnant air,

Seems to proclaim thy might is working there!

Is it that thy supernal energy,

Condens'd below, is lab'ring to be free;

And in earth's subterranean caverns pent,

Tosses and rends the globe to find a vent ?
As some etherial spirit bursts the chain,
That bound it struggling in the frenzied brain ?

Oft' from the regions of the sunless sky,
Th' electric fluid, sporting, meets the eye ;
Shooting in meteors through the arch of night ;
Crossing the darkness with a thread of light ;
As if some fairy hand were scattering there
Her shining shafts, at random, through the air ;
While from his hand some mightier being hurl'd
Vast balls of fire, that flash upon the world ;
Whose greater light illumes the scene below ;
Beneath whose transient blaze the waters glow :
Waking from its repose the forest dark,
While the plain glitters in the bursting spark ;
Which swift dispers'd in thousand fragments round,
Leaves the succeeding darkness more profound.
When midnight spreads above her sable pall,
And blackness, deep and dread, envelopes all ;
The wild and awful gleam appears to show
A fiery demon flashing wrath and woe ;
Whose eye-balls roll in flame—whose fearful form
Seems borne on clouds, and pillow'd on the storm :

As if let loose to smite the world with death;
And poison nature with its baleful breath.

When the bold vessel climbs the northern main,
Where rigid winter holds her iron reign;
The northern meteor sheds its fluttering light,
And mounts in shining pillars o'er the night;
In fitful flashes starts upon the view,
Varying in tint from pale to blood-red hue:
Now bursting as from out some sable cloud,
Fringing with light its intervening shroud;
That melts in various colours from the gaze,
Like those that catch the evening's parting rays—
In obelisks of flame now towering high;
Now in a glowing arch that cuts the sky;
Changing, as swiftly as the eye can mark,
Its Protean forms that wanton in the dark:
Making earth light, when Sol is far away,
It yields the world in sport a transient day;
And oft with all the tints that mark the noontide ray.
Where reigns the lengthen'd midnight of the pole,
Wrapping in tedious gloom the wearied soul;
Th' Aurora sheds its welcome beams around,
To break the darkness lingering and profound:

Illumes the icy isles that sail the deep ;
And pictures Hudson's Bay in ample sweep ;
And guides the traveller over Lapland snows :
Where vegetation droops in long repose :
Sparkling as if the heavens were arch'd with gems,
Profusely set in glitt'ring diadems—
In shapes so wild, that oft the wond'ring eye
Might fancy demons battling in the sky !
Whence superstition seldom fails to find,
Omens of evil to affright the mind ;
And in those fiery armies of the air,
Sees famine, war, and plague predicted there.

Death ! thou mysterious and terrific power—
How doth thy feast the young—the strong devour !
Thy shafts unseen—invisible—alike
The manly form and aged bosom strike.
Behold the lifeless limb, whose muscles show
The strength that never shrank from other foe :
Fix'd like the curling wave, that, as it roll'd,
Congeal'd, arrested by the touch of cold :
So doth thy deadly, iron grasp, suspend
The warmth, the motion, thou hast doom'd to end.
Motion, the first—last—certain proof of life ;

Whether display'd in rapture, love, or strife—

What power, when thou hast check'd it, can impart

Movement to limb—vibration to the heart?

That mystic throb that stays not night nor day,

From birth to death, in joy or grief to play.

Lying like marble statue on its bier;

And as insensible to hope or fear—

Whose fiat shall command that form again

To stir—to start—as in delight or pain?

Whose voice, save the Almighty's, lift those pale,

Fix'd—frozen eyelids from the orbs they veil?

Yes—ev'n this wonder strikes our sense the while

The corse is touch'd by the Galvanic pile;

When the cold nerves the potent fluid own:

And death seems almost shaken from his throne!

See! the eyes move—they tremble—they unclose!

As if awaking from their long repose!

Their stony orbs glare hideous on the sight—

Yet see not—nor reflect one beam of light!

They open but to mock the useless ray

That seems on their sepulchral balls to play—

They move—but never shall awake to send

One speaking glance to eye of foe or friend.

Behold! the corse uprears its lifeless arm,

As if it sought to work some deed of harm!
The very heart seems panting in its seat,
As gifted with a second life to beat—
The lips—the cheeks—appear convuls'd again—
As if not yet beyond the reach of pain:
As though some conscious passion struggled there;
And yet it hath endured life's last—despair.
The quiv'ring limbs seem starting into life;
To wage with death another useless strife;
As if there were some power that still might save,
And give to flesh a hope beyond the grave:
To force the spirit from its place of rest,
Once more to burst in anguish from the breast—
Recall'd in mockery, where hope was not,
To flee again—and be again forgot.

When like a small dark cloud that sails on high,
The only object in th' expanse of sky;
Some solitary vessel breasts the main,
Where desolation seems to hold her reign—
Where cries for help, whatever woes assail,
Must die unanswer'd on the passing gale—
Far from all land where human hand might aid;
By hope forsaken, and by fate betray'd—

Who can depict the mariner's despair,
Who sees his bark, his sole reliance there ;
Smitten by lightning in its fiercest ire ;
And bursting out in flames of quenchless fire ;
And shedding o'er the waves its awful ray,
Himself of either element the prey !
His only refuge the unfathom'd deep—
Death in the burning bark—or desperate leap !
Can language paint his anguish, as he sees
The flames swift spreading in the fanning breeze,
While driven from spot to spot they close him round,
Till not a plank to bear his foot is found :
He strains his eye across the dark blue wave,
In hope some vessel may approach to save—
But finds an utter blank on every side !
He sees the arch'd horizon meet the tide ;
But nothing—nothing that to him can give
The faintest hope an hour shall see him live.
In desperation wild, he thinks of those
Far absent friends, in safety and repose ;
And deems perchance, ev'n then they pour the prayer,
For his return—whose doom is sealing there !
The flames approach—they reach—they scorch his brow !
His mind resolves—no choice is left him now—

But in the deep to seek a milder death,
And in the world of waters yield his breath!
Perchance more kind, the spark at once may fly,
To where the stores of warlike powder lie—
Then one dread flash illumes the startled tide—
The vessel, rent like flax on every side,
In thousand fragments floats upon the waves,
As if to mark her recent inmates' graves.
Death comes—but does not stay to shake his dart—
Before 'tis seen—the life has left the heart!
'Tis not a doom of ling'ring—harrowing woe:
When fear shrinks back—but cannot shun the blow:
It does not wake one passion from its rest;
But like a light extinguish'd leaves the breast.
The spirit is not slowly wrench'd away,
Loth to forsake its tenement of clay;
Trembling to launch upon the dread unknown—
'Tis one half-instant shock—and all is done!
A moment past—a vessel bounded there,
With sails and colours glitt'ring in the air;
In giant bulk, with more than living pride,
She dash'd the surge aside, and spurn'd the tide!
And there were living men, who saw with glee
How safe she bore them o'er th' unfathom'd sea:

And from her decks laughter and shouts arose,
From hundreds who defied all mortal foes;
And in her bosom there were living things,
Horses and kine, and fowls with untried wings;
And stores the hand of toil had wrought for gain—
She seem'd a town transported o'er the main!
A moment past—she thus was proudly seen—
A mighty object sea and sky between—
The lightning flash'd—the thunder o'er her past;
There was a sudden crash—a fiery blast—
A smoke envelop'd her—it roll'd away—
Some scatter'd fragments on the billows lay—
And save those fragments, there was nothing more
Left of the ship, nor of the freight she bore!
And Oh! if Science can arrest this spark,
And lead it harmless through the rescued bark;
If she can save those hundred beings there
From death—and those who love them from despair—
Then does she give the brightest—noblest gem
That ever graced a mortal's diadem!
At once the glory and the friend of man,
She forms his highest boast since time began.

END OF ELECTRICITY.

STANZAS.

1.

Loved Harp! I do not say farewell to thee,
As Poets erst have said, who meant it not:
Thou sole kind soother of my destiny;
With whom the pangs of life I oft' forgot;
If fate, in her dark will, should e'er decree
Our separation—then she seals my lot—
Hope from that instant sets no more to rise,
Nor earth with all her scenes show aught to charm
    mine eyes.

2.

Not yet farewell—not yet—I have but tried
To wake thy chords with rude and feeble hand;
Untaught in all that form'd my joy and pride:
Fain would I hope to pour a sound more grand;
Now more advent'rous, since so rich a tide
Of harmony hath thrill'd my native land;
And raised it to that rapture with the strain,
That bard untutor'd scarce can hope to wake again.

3.

Would I resign thee! not for all that earth,
Known or unknown, contains within her womb;
No! not to stand the first of princely birth;
The highest—richest sublunary doom,
Without thee were a prize of little worth;
Or having lost thee—but a gilded tomb!
Who once has known the thrill of mental joy,
Would rather life should close, than fate that boon
    destroy.

4.

I will—must cherish thee; for thou hast been
The sweet beguiler of full many an hour,
When withering darkness, closing o'er the scene,
Had sunk me else beyond hope's saving power:
By thee recall'd, she shone the clouds between,
That, while I touch'd thee, seem'd no more to lour—
Care—sorrow—fortune's frowns—all past away;
And through the wintry gloom there burst a sunny ray.

5.

Though in those hours of darkness and of sorrow,

I swept thy chords with scarcely conscious hand;

Though midnight lent no hope to cheer the morrow,

And nought but shapes of woe my spirit scann'd—

Still—still—from thee alone I seem'd to borrow

Some nameless charm to cheer life's wildering land:

It beam'd like friendship 'midst the dungeon's gloom;

To wing the captive's hours, and mitigate his doom.

6.

Oh! could I hope to other ears thy strain

Might yield but half the joy it gave to me—

To know I had not touch'd thee quite in vain—

To live, when dead, in some kind memory—

'Twould smooth the passage through this track of

    pain;

And blunt the sharpest sting of destiny.

'Twas all I sigh'd for—all I now can hope—

My fancy's fondest dream—ambition's widest scope.

THE END.

LONDON :

Printed by D. S. Maurice, Fenchurch Street.

Lightning Source UK Ltd.
Milton Keynes UK
UKHW02n0828190818
327370UK00002B/77/P